GOD'S
NEW
ENVOYS

BOOKS EXPLORING FRESH INSIGHTS
FOR COMMUNICATING THE GOSPEL
IN TOMORROW'S DIFFERENT WORLD

DONALD K. SMITH, GENERAL EDITOR

Donald K. Smith, a thirty-year veteran of missionary service in Africa, is general director of the Institute for International Christian Communication. Dr. Smith also chairs the Department of World Ministry at Western Seminary in Portland, Oregon.

GOD'S NEW ENVOYS

A BOLD STRATEGY FOR PENETRATING "CLOSED COUNTRIES"

TETSUNAO YAMAMORI

MULTNOMAH · PRESS

Portland, Oregon 97266

Author royalties from the sale of this book have been designated for the relief and development work of Food for the Hungry, Inc. These funds will support symbiotic ministry to help fight the two hungers—of the body and of the soul.

Cover design by Bruce DeRoos
Interior design and charts by Lois Kent Davis

GOD'S NEW ENVOYS
© 1987 by Multnomah Press
Portland, Oregon 97266

Multnomah Press is a ministry of Multnomah School of the Bible, 8435 NE Glisan Street, Portland, OR 97220

Printed in the United States of America

Library of Congress Cataloging-in-Publication Data

Yamamori, Tetsunao, 1937-
  God's new envoys.

  Bibliography: p.
  1. Missions—Theory. 2. Twenty-first century—
Forecasts. I. Title.
BV2063.Y36   1987   266   86-31258
ISBN: 0-88070-188-9

87 88 89 90 91 92 93 – 10 9 8 7 6 5 4 3 2 1

AFFECTIONATELY DEDICATED

TO DONALD AND MARY MCGAVRAN

It is not often that the complexity of today's mission task is laid out with such clarity and simplicity. This is a book pastors and lay leaders will want to pick up and read from cover to cover.

> John C. Bennett
> Former Executive Director
> Association of Church Missions Committees

God's New Envoys . . . addresses squarely the tremendous challenge the Church faces in reaching the 3.3 billion non-Christians.

> Clyde Cook
> President
> Biola University

Dr. Yamamori has done a great service in writing this timely book on the strategic work Christian laity can perform in world evangelization.

> J. Christy Wilson, Jr.
> Professor of World Evangelization
> Gordon-Conwell Theological Seminary

C O N T E N T S

MAPS, CHARTS, AND DIAGRAMS

F O R E W O R D

"THE Evangelization of the World in This Generation . . ." The year 1988 marks the one-hundredth anniversary of the Student Volunteer Movement which sounded that stirring slogan as a trumpet call to summon an army of young Christian visionaries to the task of world evangelization. The Church today is the beneficiary of their herculean labors.

That same challenge still confronts us, but the obstacles and adversaries may seem more formidable—repressive Marxism, resurgent Islam and other world faiths, and pervasive secularism. The doors to some nations appear to be firmly closed, and doors to others are closing. In many lands where traditional missionaries still are permitted, their activities are restricted.

The author of this book points out that as the twenty-first century dawns, a projected 83 percent of the world's non-Christian population will reside in countries closed to traditional missionary approaches. He correctly describes that development as "a deeply disturbing trend."

He stresses as equally disturbing the fact that we currently deploy less than ten percent of the world's Christian missionary force and five percent of mission funds for cross-cultural outreach to those people groups in which there is no viable indigenous church capable of evangelizing them. That situation, he contends, calls for fervent prayer, renewed commitment, new vision, and innovative strategy.

The author, an esteemed evangelical leader, is himself a product of cross-cultural and missionary outreach to Japan where his family had a Shintoist/Buddhist background. His conversion, his splendid academic training, and subsequent service as president of Food for the Hungry have equipped him to address this issue. He advances here a thrilling new vision and a breathtaking, workable strategy.

He calls for recruitment and deployment of an army of "God's New Envoys" to supplement the efforts of traditional missionaries. Many parts of the world that are closed to traditional missionaries urgently need and welcome trained teachers, medical personnel, engineers, business leaders, agriculturists, and other specialists. Christians who have expertise in those fields, he maintains, should be hearing the call of God to volunteer.

The concept of "tentmakers" is not a new one; but here is a systematic, feasible, well-developed strategy for the training and deployment of such tentmakers or new envoys.

This book offers a careful analysis of requirements for such work and suggested training for it. Specific case studies are cited to demonstrate the effectiveness of that approach.

The Church is in debt to Dr. Yamamori for this contribution to missiology. The concept of God's lay ambassadors will be the topic of careful consideration at the International Congress on World Evangelization which the Lausanne movement will sponsor in 1989.

This valuable book exhibits sound scriptural principles, cultural sensitivity, and a practical orientation. It exhorts the rousing call of a century ago, and offers a practical strategy to further the vision of the evangelization of the world in this generation.

Leighton Ford
Charlotte, North Carolina
August 1986

ACKNOWLEDGMENTS

I wish to thank ISSACHAR Frontier Missions Research and especially research associate Andrew D. Jackson for timely and helpful compilation of the list of countries (in chapter 2) to which missionary access is restricted. Thanks also are due to Doug Millham of World Vision who compiled the list (in chapter 12) of recommended schools. Both these lists were generously provided in advance of planned publication elsewhere.

As we prepare to face the challenge of mobilizing for the twenty-first-century mission, I would additionally like to thank David Barrett and the team of five hundred researchers who compiled the mammoth *World Christian Encyclopedia* (Oxford Press, 1982), as well as all the other researchers worldwide whose work is dedicated to giving us more knowledge for use in planning strategies in the essential task of world evangelization.

Finally, I am deeply grateful to Doug Jardine of Doug Ross Communications, without whose expert editorial assistance the publication of this present volume would have been delayed.

W A N T E D :

100,000 New Envoys
to serve in countries
closed to traditional missionaries.

No salary. No security.
Hardship, danger expected.
Special training, new strategies required.

Immediate Need!

INTRODUCTION

WHEN the twenty-first century begins, an estimated *83 percent* of the world's non-Christian population will reside in countries closed to traditional missionary approaches.

This book proposes new strategies for reaching these approximately 3.5 billion "unreachable" people.[1] It also proposes a challenging new vocation for those called to the missions field.

In these pages you'll meet a new breed of missionaries. I call them God's New Envoys. You'll learn about their qualifications, their training, and the strategies they employ. Possibly you'll feel moved to join their ranks or to encourage others to do so.

It is not this book's intent that the number of traditional missionaries be reduced. I hope rather that their ranks will be increased in concert with the fielding of these new missionaries, God's New Envoys, who can minister to the 3.5 billion people whom traditional missionary approaches can no longer effectively reach.

The goal, as always, is obedience to our Lord's "Great Commission":

> "Be my witnesses . . . to the ends of the earth" (Acts 1:8), to "go into all the world and preach the good news to all creation" (Mark 16:15), and to "go and make disciples of all nations, baptizing them in the name of the Father and of the Son and of the Holy Spirit, and teaching them to obey everything I have commanded you" (Matthew 28:19-20).[2]

There is no ignoring the binding and urgent nature of these commands. So one additional objective of this book is to mobilize Christians who have mistakenly seen the Great Commission as voluntary.

This book is intended primarily for . . .

- students, professionals, and other skilled and dedicated people who might qualify to join the ranks of God's New Envoys.
- pastors, ministers, teachers, missions executives, and others who are charged to encourage and counsel those planning missionary careers.
- all those concerned with Christian relief and development work—who seek better ways to meet physical needs while increasing the harvest for Christ.

Finally, I have written this book to assist the nearly three hundred thousand traditional missionaries who now labor in the field so valiantly.[3] I hope they will find some of these New Envoy strategies adaptable to make their own harvesting more abundant and their own strategies more clear.

Throughout these pages you'll find examples of God's New Envoys in action, illustrating different situations they will encounter and the kinds of strategies they can employ. These examples are drawn from case studies of traditional missionaries who, in the situations illustrated, are responding as New Envoys would in the face of such challenges.

All the examples are based on the experiences of real missionaries in real-world situations. The occasional improvisation of names and locations is intended to protect missionaries and converts now in restricted lands.

A PERSONAL WORD

As you journey through this book, you may find it helpful to know a little more about the author who accompanies you.

To begin, you should know that the topics discussed in this book are profoundly important to me. In different forms they have been the focus of my entire career.

Over the past thirty years I have been studying church growth and missions strategies, first as a student, then as a university professor, and also by writing about them in more than thirty articles and books.

Recently my involvement in global evangelism has taken a different turn. Currently I lead a Christian relief and development organization, the goal of which is to minister in our Lord's name to the physical and spiritual hungers of suffering people in desperately needy areas of the world.

This experience, like the ones before, has strengthened my conviction that the Great Commission can be pursued with far greater effectiveness.

I am sure that part of the motivation for this book, as in all my missions writings, comes from the fact that I myself was once counted among the "foreign" nonbelievers we seek to reach. Thus, for me, the needs of the unreached will always be very real, as will their pain.

In my case, that pain became acute the last year of World War II, when I was seven and lived in Japan's third largest city, Nagoya. I was a Buddhist and Shintoist then, taught by my parents to look for support to the Lord Buddha, to nature spirits, and to my ancestors. During that time I watched three bombs hit our property, saw a family member killed, and began to think deeply about human suffering and the possibility for true world peace.

At that time I also experienced physical hunger. Like some of those described in this book, I was one of the millions of children whose food supply was disrupted by war. In fact, if the shortages in Nagoya had continued much longer, I probably would have died.

The memories of that physical and spiritual hunger and of the deadly effects of war never left me. They remain strong even today.

After things got better, I attended Jesuit schools—respected in my country for their high educational standards. I was still, however, not a believer.

Then another war—this time in Korea—brought a United States Air Force chaplain to Nagoya. As I got to know the Vernon Kullowatz family, I began thinking there was something different about them, these Christians from America.

Through this family I began attending church. I wanted to know more about the God who sent Jesus Christ. I also volunteered to work for the Kullowatzes as a houseboy, to see if their belief was practiced at home. (It was.)

Soon, I started reading a Bible the Kullowatzes had given me. I also began preparing to study law, seeking a career in the diplomatic corps where I hoped to make a contribution to world peace.

As with most conversions, the rest is something of a mystery. I came to understand that the diplomatic corps was not the answer—and that the only lasting peace for the world would come as "we have peace with God through our Lord Jesus Christ" (Romans 5:1).

While at Nanzan University in Nagoya, I discovered I wanted to learn more about God's Word, to learn to be a "workman . . . who correctly handles the word of truth" (2 Timothy 2:15). The first step, I knew, was to establish "vertical" peace through a direct saving relationship with God in Jesus Christ. Only after that, I believed, could the true "horizontal" peace follow, in which neighbors love neighbors as themselves.

Having at last discovered my direction, there was no stopping. I studied the Bible in one college, received a divinity degree from another, became a Christian minister, and completed a doctorate in sociology of religion. This led to the teaching, writing, and Christian relief work.

Then came the present endeavor—which you and I can pursue together on the following pages, as we explore new strategies and a new mobilization of manpower for the twenty-first-century mission.

Documentation and Notes

1. The 83 percent and 3.5 billion estimates were derived from computations using the 77 restricted-access countries identified by ISSACHAR Frontier Missions Research, as well as projections for the non-Christian populations of these same countries in David B. Barrett, ed., *World Christian Encyclopedia: A Comparative Study of Churches and Religions in the Modern World, AD 1900 to 2000* (Nairobi: Oxford University Press, 1982), pp. 133-771. Chapter 2 will provide a breakdown of this information.

Since it is unknowable precisely which countries will be restricted to traditional missionary approaches in the year 2000, my calculations are based on the assumption that the same 77 countries will still be restricted fourteen years from now, and do not even include the seven "emerging restrictive" countries cited by ISSACHAR.

These projections, it seems to me, are quite conservative. The total population of non-Christians in restricted countries or people groups could well turn out to be greater than the 3.5 billion we have assumed.

2. As shown on the back of the title page, Scripture quotations in this book are taken from the *New International Version*. For the convenience of readers, however, scriptural references will always be provided within the text, so readers can readily make comparison with the version of their choice.

3. Barrett, *World Christian Encyclopedia*, p. 17.

THE MANDATE FOR THE GLOBAL MISSION

THE fundamental reason for God's New Envoys is that increasingly large areas of the world are no longer accessible to the traditional missionary approaches of the past.

A century ago the situation looked much rosier. From the late 1800s through the first few years of the 1900s, many missions strategists believed the world could be evangelized before the twentieth century drew to a close. David B. Barrett in the *World Christian Encyclopedia* states:

> By the year 1900, one third of humanity were Christians, and one half were aware of Christianity and had become influenced by it. Optimism for rapid completion of the task of global evangelization was high. From 1889 to 1914 the great Protestant and Anglican communions of Europe and North America promoted the Watchword that summarized this optimism in the objective "The Evangelization of the World in This Generation."[1]

Sadly, these optimistic projections have not been realized. Today, nearly a century later, the total percentage of the world's population identified as Christian has actually declined. In 1900, the best estimate of professing Christians was 34.4 percent of the global population, an all-time high.[2] This declined to 33.7 percent in 1970 and to 33.2 percent in 1975, still further to 32.4 percent in 1985, and is projected by Barrett to drop an additional tenth of a percentage point to 32.3 percent in the year 2000.[3]

As we face the end of our own century, it's essential we understand why our recent missions efforts have not achieved the goals which many optimistically predicted would be attainable well before now. Even more importantly, we need to examine the new emerging barriers which, if uncircumvented, will make global evangelism even more tenuous in the twenty-first century.

But before looking into these, we need to take two other steps: first, to define our terms, so we can focus our investigation more precisely; second, to review why we should devote our time, and perhaps even our lives, to evangelizing in foreign lands.

DEFINITION OF TERMS

In almost any discussion of this subject, a handful of important words tend to be used repeatedly, words describing parts of the process central to this book's purpose—bringing people outside one's homeland to faith and obedience in Christ. Brief definitions of these terms will be sufficient for us here.

The first, *evangelization,* is specifically related to proclamation of the gospel. According to the helpful definition in the *World Christian Encyclopedia,* being evangelized refers to "the state of having the good news spread or offered; the state of being aware of Christianity, Christ and the gospel."[4]

Evangelism, for our purposes, does *not* mean conversion. Rather, it would seem to be exactly what Jesus had in mind when He told the disciples to "Go into all the world and preach the good news to all creation" (Mark 16:15).

An evangelized people is one in which more than half the members have had an opportunity to hear or read some of the key elements in the gospel. They have not necessarily been converted.

A second concept has to do with whether or not a people group is *reached*. To qualify as reached, there must be a viable indigenous church capable of evangelizing within that people group.

The word "indigenous" here is key. The indigenous church or Christ group is self-sufficient, and thus can continue without outside support.

Most important of all, a reached group can potentially have the local resources to maintain and expand its Christian population, even in highly restrictive environments such as those where many of God's New Envoys might work.[5]

The concept of a *Christ group* is used in this book to cover indigenous churches, as well as house churches and other secret gatherings of Christians which often must be the church alternatives in the "closed countries" where New Envoys will be sent.[6]

For our purposes, *people groups* are best defined as culturally and linguistically separate peoples (such as the Maasai tribes of Kenya or the Hmong hill tribes of Laos). By some definitions there are 24,000 such people groups in the world today, about 17,000 of which have still not been reached. These 17,000 are the unreached people groups, or "hidden peoples," estimated in mid-1985 to comprise more than 2.5 billion human beings.[7]

Throughout this book, the word *closed* will be used to refer to the people groups and countries to which traditional missionaries cannot gain access without disguising their true vocation and purpose. The 77 countries and thousands of people groups which are currently closed tend to be predominantly in the Muslim and Communist world.[8]

Another basic concept is *conversion*. In Matthew 28:19 Jesus says, "Go and make disciples of all nations, baptizing them in the name of the Father and of the Son and of the Holy

Spirit." In other cases baptism is not mentioned, and the instructions are to accept the Lord Jesus Christ as Savior, possibly through a special prayer, public proclamation of faith, or some other means.

To avoid disputes about when precisely conversion takes place, I prefer a more global concept—that of *bringing people to faith and obedience in Christ*. This term is quite precise and, it seems to me, describes our objective very well. The only problem, of course, is that it is unmeasurable and unquantifiable, except of course to God. Thus, throughout this book we will sometimes be forced to quantify the concept of conversion in less precise terms.

In many statistical cases, for example, we will talk about "professing" Christians—thereby basing the number of Christians on the number of individuals who claim the title of Christian as their own.

Through the years we have struggled to find better ways to count Christians in comparison to the national or international population at large. I generally prefer to use the term *communicants* (adult church members). This category is less elastic than the term "communities," which some denominations (Roman Catholics, for example) prefer, and which includes not only adult members of a given church but also their children, who certainly tend to be influenced by their parents' religious preference.

By converting all our figures whenever possible to communicants, we avoid the error of attempting to compare incomparables.

This is probably a good time to make another distinction, necessitated by the fact that there is currently a net increase of 270 new Christian denominations throughout the world each year. As of this writing, the number of denominations and church groups totals more than 22,000, all claiming to be the best way to follow the Way of Christ.[9] With this broad range of sometimes competing denominations, I want to clarify that the goal of this book is to help bring more people to faith and obedience in Christ, not to any particular denomination or group of denominations within the global Body of Christ.

I am confident that once the new convert has moved to faith and obedience, she or he will be properly guided as is required, by the greatest Teacher of all. Perhaps the best recent example of this is the explosive growth of the Church in China after the expulsion of the missionaries.

This is not to say I lack personal convictions about ways of worship and interpretations of God's Word. These matters are of vital concern to me, as they are to most Christians. The burden of this book, however, is to develop strategies that can help bring hundreds of millions more people to Christ—and not to dispute about fine points of doctrine, however important, with those who are already believers.

Our goal is to build up the Body of Christ and to expand His Church, not to weaken it through additional factional squabbles at a time when the salvation of billions depends on our working as one. Together as His Church, the Body of all faithful believers, we are charged to pursue *the Church's mission:* to proclaim Christ and bring all people possible to faith and obedience in Him (Romans 16:26).

RATIONALE FOR EVANGELISM ABROAD

Now that necessary definitions have been briefly spelled out, it's time to take the next step: to explore why we should be so audacious, and often so self-sacrificing, as to leave the comfort and security of our homelands to pursue evangelism abroad.

Many of the reasons for this are very old. Others are quite new, necessitated in recent years by changes in populations and governments. Although these reasons are written here primarily for an audience in the more developed world, it should be noted that most of them will also have relevance to the less developed world, which is now expanding its own Christian missions outreach at a very rapid rate.[10]

Here are eight basic reasons for continuing and expanding our evangelism abroad—or, if you prefer, our *global mission:*

1. *Because Christ mandated the global mission*—in Acts 1:8, Mark 16:15, and Matthew 28:19-20. Elsewhere He reinforces these instructions in different words:

> Come, follow me . . . and I will make you fishers of men. (Matthew 4:19)

> The Christ will suffer and rise from the dead on the third day, and repentance and forgiveness of sins will be preached in his name *to all nations.* (Luke 24:46-47)

> I tell you, open your eyes and look at the fields! They are ripe for harvest. (John 4:35)

> As the Father has sent me, I am sending you. (John 20:21)

And finally, the instructions to Peter:

> Feed my lambs. . . . Take care of my sheep. . . . Feed my sheep. (John 21:15-17)

2. *Because our Lord appears to establish global evangelism as a precondition of His return.* In Matthew 24:14 He says,

> And this gospel of the kingdom will be preached in the whole world as a testimony to all nations, *and then the end will come.*

Later, in Revelation 5:9-10, the risen Lord Jesus is addressed as one who

> purchased men for God from every tribe and language and people and nation.

3. *Because as Christians we have received a precious gift which must be shared as widely as possible.* Put simply, if we are called to share our food, our cloaks, our shelter—which are only temporal things—how much more should we be called to share our greatest gift, the faith which provides eternal life?

4. *Because every individual is important . . . and every*

individual's spiritual hunger deserves to be met. Clearly John
3:16 emphasizes this divine intent of universal access to salvation:

> For God so loved the world that He gave his one and only
> Son, that whoever believes in him shall not perish, but
> have eternal life.

As long as we are alive and have breath in our lungs, those
of us who have already heard the good news must continue to
expend a portion of that breath to witness, so more of God's children can be saved.

5. *Because if we don't win those of our global neighbors
who hunger for change, other less desirable forces will.* Increasingly we see human hunger and need providing an opening for
evil forces to move in. To see this truth, we need only to look at
the rapid fashion that Communism and non-Christian religions
filled the spiritual vacuum in many former colonial African nations since 1960.

Spiritual hunger, in my opinion, is basic to the human condition. God Himself creates spiritual hunger in every person.
The Lord God says in Amos 8:11, "The time is surely coming
. . . when I will send a famine on the land—not a famine of
bread or water, but of hearing the words of the Lord" (*Living
Bible*). Once that hunger is aroused, or—more accurately—
once a person is made aware of its existence, the need will be
filled somehow, by whichever religion or ideology is most per-
suasively represented to the person who hungers. Conversely, if
Christianity is not effectively represented in the area when that
hunger is experienced, the opening may pass forever.

6. *Because Christianity's adversaries are increasingly
ruthless.* If you are a resident of Canada, Europe, Japan, the
United States, or some other more developed, democratic nation, it's frequently hard to grasp the true evil of some of the
alternatives to Christianity—religions and quasi-religions—
which also vie for uncommitted hearts and souls. For many parts
of the world, this alternative "religion" is Communism.

Elsewhere it may be voodoo, or religions that subject adherents to drastic forms of discrimination and even direct physical abuse.

In recent history, the wanton murder of hundreds of thousands of Christians in Uganda by Idi Amin, and the systematic torture and cruel imprisonment of the faithful in Vietnam under the guise of "reeducation" show the steps hostile governments are willing to take regardless of public opinion.

7. *Because only changed lives can change society, and only a changed global society can truly live in peace.* This is a personal favorite of mine, because it relates to my conviction since my conversion three decades ago that we can achieve "horizontal" peace in the world only as we increasingly, one-by-one, achieve "vertical" peace with God. On a practical level, there is surely no doubt that some of Christianity's strongest global competitors teach violence and strife: militant, fundamentalist Islam, dictatorial Communism, anarchism, and of course the many quasi-religious forms of terrorism which permeate our world.

8. *Because Christian missionary work, in its many forms, is still one of the satisfying adventures of all.* Never doubt the sheer excitement of working in foreign countries to help others find salvation.

These then are the eight reasons, any of which would be sufficient justification for pursuing global evangelization through our financial support, through our prayers, and through actual service abroad.

To summarize: We need to reach out to the non-Christian population abroad . . .

- because it's biblically right.
- because we care about these people and their salvation.
- because if we delay, billions of non-Christians may lose not only their chance of eternal salvation, but their opportunities for more satisfying lives here and now.

These, then, are the reasons all Christians should support the most vigorous possible evangelization effort to all parts of the world.

Next question: Is that goal being achieved?

QUESTIONS FOR THOUGHT AND REVIEW

• Why are New Envoys needed at this time?
• What's the difference between the "unreached" people and "unreachable" people (those living in restricted-access countries)?
• Give five reasons why you feel global evangelism is required.

Documentation and Notes

1. Barrett, *World Christian Encyclopedia*, p. 3.
2. By A.D. 500, 22.4 percent of the world is believed to have been Christian. This dropped to 19 percent in 1500, then rose to 23.1 percent in 1800.
3. Barrett, p. 4.
4. Barrett, p. 826.
5. John A. Holzmann, "1.3 Billion 'UNEVANGELIZED' or 2.4 Billion 'UNREACHED,'" in *Mission Frontiers*, August/September 1985, p. 21.
6. The concept of "openness" and ways it can be measured will be discussed in some detail in chapter 6.
7. Ralph D. Winter, *Mission Frontiers*, August/September 1985, p. 3.
8. The total numbers of closed countries and closed people groups vary from source to source. A list of restricted-access countries which is current as of this writing is included in chapter 2.
9. Barrett, p. 17.
10. Barrett, p. 17.

C H A P T E R 2

THE UNFINISHED TASK IS GROWING

THERE are now more non-Christians on this earth than at any time since the world began.

And unless a profound and dramatic change in our global evangelization process takes place, this huge mass of unsaved humanity will grow *even larger*—from the entirely unacceptable total of 3.3 billion non-Christians in mid-1985, to 4.2 billion people in the year 2000 who are expected to be living out their lives without knowing the Lord.[1]

This means not only that our efforts to carry the message of the gospel are ineffective, but also that they are *increasingly more ineffective*.

In one case, the failure is in evangelism—we're not spreading the Word widely and effectively enough. In another, the shortfall comes in our not reaching the unreached—we're simply not spreading the Word thoroughly enough, and thus not making disciples "of all nations" (Matthew 28:19).

Put simply, we're not succeeding at the task of bringing the gospel to those who need to hear it; and, even when we do, we're

not bringing enough of those who do hear the Word to faith and
obedience in Christ.

Knowing these two simple and rather terrifying facts gives
us a basis for analyzing why we're falling so drastically behind.
From this analysis we can begin designing a prescription for cor-
rective action.

As we explore, it's important to remember a vital fact that
separates the mission of Christ's Church from business, warfare, competitive sports, and similar worldly pursuits. The difference is that in missions, *all* efforts are productive. For there
is great benefit in the love of God expressed by every missionary's service, and a great victory with every new human being
brought to Christ.

We are not failures in our missions effort just because of
the enormous 3.3-billion-person gap between our objective in
obeying the Great Commission and the results we've actually
achieved. The point is that *every* effort is important in bringing
people to faith and obedience in Christ, and no man or woman's
career in missions can be deemed a failure—or, for that matter,
less than glorious—just because the numbers of converts are
less than they might be.

However, as we involve more servants of Christ in the
wonderful endeavor of sharing the good news, we will accelerate, with God's help, the accomplishment of the Great Commission our Lord gave us.

Having said that, it's time to take a careful look at our
world, exploring important emerging factors that have contrib-
uted to the rapid expansion of the world's non-Christian population, and the increasing difficulty of reaching them.

POPULATION GROWTH

The world's population has grown rapidly since the days
of optimistic projections by nineteenth-century missions
strategists—and it will continue to do so.

WHERE ARE THE WORLD'S NON-CHRISTIANS?

. . . in 1985:

2.7 billion in *closed* countries
(roughly 2.3 *unreached*, and .4 *reached*)

.6 billion in *open* countries
(roughly .2 *unreached*, and .4 *reached*)

. . . in 2000:

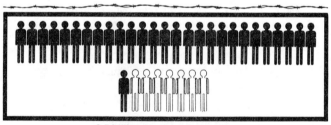

3.5 billion in *closed* countries
(roughly 2.8 *unreached*, and .7 *reached*)

.7 billion in *open* countries
(roughly .3 *unreached*, and .4 *reached*)

KEY

= members of *unreached* people groups (2.5 billion in 2000)

closed = not freely accessible by traditional missionaries

= members of *reached* people groups

unreached = not having a viable, indigenous church capable of evangelizing within the people group

All figures estimated and rounded off.

RESTRICTED COUNTRIES
Based on Religious Freedom and Accessibility
(Population figures are estimates
for the year 2000)

1. **TOTALLY RESTRICTED**
   (3 countries: Albania, Mongolia, North Korea)

   Total population: 34,621,000
   Total non-Christians: 34,291,000

2. **EXTREMELY RESTRICTED**
   (23 countries: Afghanistan, Bhutan, Bulgaria, Cuba, Czechoslovakia, Ethiopia, Iran, Iraq, Kampuchea, Kuwait, Laos, Libya, Mauritania, North Yemen, Qater, Romania, Saudi Arabia, Somalia, South Yemen, Soviet Union, Syria, Turkey, Vietnam)

   Total population: 806,978,000
   Total non-Christians: 602,625,000

3. **HIGHLY RESTRICTED**
   (20 countries: Algeria, Angola, Bahrain, Benin, Burma, China, Comoros, East Germany, Egypt, Guinea, Hungary, Malaysia, Maldives, Morocco, Mozambique, Nepal, Oman, Poland, Sudan, Uganda)

   Total population: 1,544,152,000
   Total non-Christians: 1,422,620,000

4. **MODERATELY RESTRICTED**
   (31 countries: Bangladesh, Brunei, Burundi, Cape Verde Islands, Central African Republic, Chad, Congo, Equatorial Guinea, Greece, Guinea-Bissau, Guyana, India, Israel, Jordan, Madagascar, Mali, Malta, Nicaragua, Niger, Pakistan, Sao Tome & Principe, Seychelles, Sri Lanka, Suriname, Thailand, Togo, Tunisia, United Arab Emirates, Yugoslavia, Zaire, Zimbabwe)

   Total population: 1,652,148,000
   Total non-Christians: 1,474,703,000

5. **EMERGING RESTRICTIONS**
   (7 countries: Chile, Colombia, Costa Rica, Lebanon, Mexico, Panama, Taiwan)

   Total population: 236,771,000
   Total non-Christians: 35,480,000

World population at the time of Jesus' birth has been estimated at 300 million. It reached 1.6 billion by 1900. By 1986
there were 4.8 billion in the world (with some well-publicized
estimates that same year showing the figure surpassing 5 billion). Projections for the years 2000 and 2020 are 6.2 billion
and 7.8 billion respectively.[2]

Approximately 32.4 percent of the world's people today
profess to be Christians. This means the remaining 67.6 percent
(3.3 billion out of 4.8 billion people) are non-Christians.

Recent and perhaps somewhat optimistic research conducted by church growth analysts indicates that this current ratio
may begin to improve in the direction of increasing the proportion of Christians in the world—with their numbers growing
possibly at a faster rate than that of the general population.

Though these reports are encouraging, they are not univer-
sally shared. Nor can even this slight improvement in the growth
rate of the Christian population be expected to reverse the
dramatic increase of the world's non-Christians, which has been
going on for most of this century.

According to David Barrett, the most comprehensive
chronicler of world Christianity to date, there will still be about
4.2 billion non-Christians out of a total population of roughly
6.2 billion in the year 2000. Applying the same percentage to
the expected population twenty years later (7.8 billion, according to the Population Reference Bureau), we get the staggering
number of 5.25 billion unsaved people in the year 2020.[3]

While some may quibble to a minor degree with some of
these projections, they lead us to an inescapable conclusion: Unless drastic changes are made in our missionary approaches, the
enormous numbers of the unsaved will continue to grow every year.

Current trends also lead us to believe that more than half
the world's 6.2 billion people in the year 2000 will be living in
cities, and 60 percent of them will be Asians. To reach the huge
number of the unsaved, we must become increasingly alert to
the importance of urban centers and to the Asian population in
particular.

INCREASING INACCESSIBILITY

Still another deeply disturbing trend characterizes the context we must prepare for in the twenty-first-century mission: the increasing inaccessibility of nations and people groups to career missionaries, as illustrated by the maps and charts in this chapter.[4]

In 1974, Ed Dayton, director of the Missions Advanced Research and Communication Center (MARC), identified 32 countries which "permitted no foreign missionaries of any type or greatly restricted evangelists within their borders."

In early 1986, a new list was produced of restricted access countries. This includes three countries that are "totally restricted," twenty-three "extremely restricted," twenty "highly restricted," and thirty-one "moderately restricted"—for a total of seventy-seven nations, with a combined mid-1985 population of approximately 3.2 billion. In addition, the list named seven other countries that displayed "emerging restrictions" to traditional missionary approaches.[5]

As can be seen, the number of people living in free or partly free countries has been on the decline. Today, 65 percent of the world's people live in countries that either partly or fully restrict traditional missionary approaches. By the year 2000, these same 77 to 84 countries are expected to continue to contain approximately 65 to 68 percent of the world's population. In addition, they are expected to contain between 83 and 84 percent of all non-Christians.

The 1985 edition of *Freedom in the World* (Freedom House of New York) takes note of the advances of Soviet Communism during the previous decade in Southeast Asia (after the fall of Vietnam), and also in South Yemen, Ethiopia, Nicaragua, and in the former Portuguese colonies of Africa. While Western Europe has experienced gains for democracy, the net result has been a decrease in the number of countries and people groups accessible to purely evangelistic missionary outreach.[6]

CULTURAL BARRIERS

Another barrier to missions outreach in the twenty-first century is the fact that growing numbers of non-Christians in closed countries live within cultural groups alien to most of the career missionaries now in the field.

Ralph Winter has expressed one dimension of this problem:

> If all the Christians in the world were to witness "across the back fence" to neighbors who spoke the same language and operated within the same cultural norms as they did, still half the world's population would remain unreached.[7]

Winter uses the term "frontier mission" to describe the cross-cultural outreach to these unreached people groups "in which there is at present no viable, indigenous, evangelizing

---

RESTRICTED COUNTRIES

Combined Population Totals

In the year 2000, in the 77 countries now classified as Totally, Extremely, Highly, or Moderately Restricted . . .

the estimated total population will be
4.0 billion

while the estimated number of non-Christians will be
3.5 billion
(or **83.4** percent of the
world's total non-Christian people)

When we include the seven additional countries now classified as having Emerging Restrictions, the estimated totals for the year 2000 are:

4.3 billion total population
3.6 billion non-Christians
(**84.2** percent of the world's total)

AFRICA

EXTREMELY RESTRICTED
Ethiopia (53.67 — 32.20)
Libya (4.74 — .12)
Mauritania (2.28 — .02)
Somalia (6.54 — .004)

HIGHLY RESTRICTED
Algeria (36.66 — .38)
Angola (12.46 — 12.09)
Benin (5.9 — 1.78)
Comoros (.4 — 0009)
Egypt (64.59 — 10.49)
Guinea (8.46 — .09)
Morocco (35.9 — .13)
Mozambique (17.65 — 8.83)
Sudan (38.98 — 4.49)
Uganda (24.16 — 20.42)

MODERATELY RESTRICTED
Burundi (7.28 — 6.95)
Cape Verde Islands (.43 — .41)
Central African Republic (3.36 — 3.06)
Chad (6.91 — 2.41)
Congo (2.72 — 2.54)
Equatorial Guinea (.497 — .437)
Guinea-Bissau (.84 — .1)
Madagascar (17.78 — 9.78)
Mali (11.26 — .28)
Niger (9.57 — .02)
Sao Tome & Principe (.088 — .087)
Togo (4.64 — 2.32)
Tunisia (10.85 — .03)
Zaire (49.45 — 47.96)
Zimbabwe (15.15 — 10.45)

(In parentheses: **first**, estimated TOTAL population for the year 2000;
second, estimated CHRISTIAN population in the year 2000.)

All figures in MILLIONS

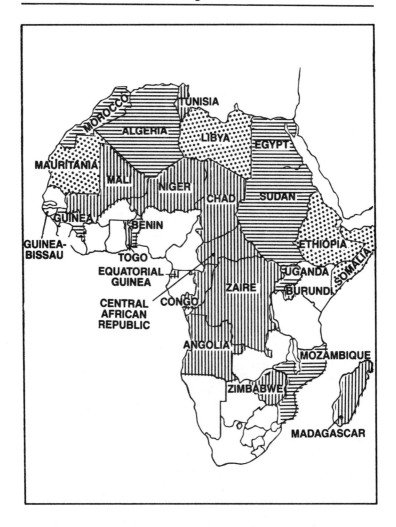

church."[8] According to this definition, about 17,000 of the world's roughly 24,000 people groups are still unreached. In 1985, this would amount to approximately 2.5 billion "unreached" or "hidden" people.

Winter states that most of the 2.5 billion unreached people are within Chinese, Hindu, Muslim, Buddhist, or tribal groups.

EASTERN EUROPE

TOTALLY RESTRICTED
Albania (4.26 — .13)

EXTREMELY RESTRICTED
Bulgaria (10.04 — 6.08)
Czechoslovakia (16.8 — 12.72)
Romania (25.76 — 20.84)
Soviet Union (315.03 — 118.1)

HIGHLY RESTRICTED
East Germany (18,23 — 10.95)
Hungary (11.07 — 9.02)
Poland (39.85 — 35.67)

MODERATELY RESTRICTED
Greece (9.62 — 9.36)
Malta (.336 — .328)
Yugoslavia (25.65 — 17.55)

(In parentheses: **first,** estimated TOTAL population for the year 2000;
second, estimated CHRISTIAN population in the year 2000.)
All figures in MILLIONS

Even more significantly, "less than 10 percent of the world's missionaries and only 5 percent of mission funds are focused on reaching these groups."[9] Though not all of the 2.5 billion unreached people are in countries closed to traditional missionaries, in most cases they are.

Perhaps, therefore, it would be worthwhile to take a closer look at three of the largest categories of peoples who tend to be among the "unreached" and who usually are found in countries where traditional missionaries are barred. This review will give some indication of the enormous potential for Christ which is currently, and regrettably, being overlooked:

* * *

Muslim nations. Most of the world's 900 million Muslims—about one-fifth of all humanity—are unreached. The opportunity here, as expressed by noted Islamic strategist J. Christy Wilson, Jr., is enormous.

Muslims today are more open to the gospel than ever, Wilson says. "In the next ten years I see a great influx of Muslims to Christ if Christians take the Great Commission seriously." Wilson also reports these heartening results:

- In Indonesia, the world's largest Muslim country, hundreds of thousands of Muslims have turned to Christ.
- Growing numbers of Muslims in Bangladesh are gathering for Bible studies.
- Seven of every ten people baptized in Iran are converted Muslims. (In fact, since Ayatollah Khomeini gained political control in 1979, "more Bibles have been bought by Iranians than in the entire history of the country.")[10]

On the other hand, Wilson notes, the consequences of not meeting this challenge could be dire: "If we don't go to the Muslims with the gospel of love, God will bring them against us in judgment. Muslim eschatology teaches that they will conquer the earth. They consider themselves in a holy war to take over the world." So the choices are: a great victory for the Lord, or continued violence for humankind.[11]

India. Though partially evangelized, India's 730 million people are substantially unreached. The world's largest democracy, India is a country with enormous needs.

It is also the birthplace of some of the world's greatest non-Christian religions. In India we have potential access to many millions of Hindus, Buddhists, Jains, Zoroastrians, and animists—among whom missionaries could refine their skills, working in relative security with a wide variety of religious and cultural groups. The challenge we face is Indian government resistance to those whose primary agenda is propagation of the faith.

China. In spite of ongoing persecution and other obstacles, China's one-billion-plus population (about twenty-three percent of the world's total) is a missions challenge that must be addressed. China also offers a special promise, in part because of the persecutions.

Carl Lawrence's book *The Church in China* contains dozens of stories of witness and hope, providing testimony to a spontaneous expansion of Christianity in one of the most unreached countries on earth.

Indigenous Christ groups continue to expand. House churches have been formed by the thousands. Believers who do not attend services in the churches that remain open instead worship in secret, in cemeteries, upper rooms, and open fields. They cannot buy Bibles, so they copy out sections of the Bible and treasure them.

Barrett in the *World Christian Encyclopedia* gives the figure of 1.8 million Christians now in China, with an expected 1.5 million Christians in the year 2000;[12] but he says these figures were based only on official government data from before 1976. More recently he estimates that 52 million people in China now profess to be Christians, and that by the turn of the century their numbers could be as high as 130 million—ten percent of China's total population![13] Christianity's growth in China, Barrett says, "is an unprecedented, massive movement that cannot be stopped."[14]

Lawrence reports that the new openness to Christ in China may be a direct result of basic practices of the Maoist Chinese Communists: "The importance of confession, self-examination, honesty before one's God/party, compassion, ideological rectitude"—all these traits were instilled by Mao.

In addition, there appears to be a high level of anxiety, a feeling of separation from one's group, a feeling of pointlessness, a feeling of despair. "Mao, though he did not plan it that way, did a good way of preparing the most populous nation in the world to receive the gospel of Jesus Christ," Lawrence says. He continues:

> Give the Chinese citizen . . . the right message—to put into that vacuum chiseled there by Mao—the message of the Person of Jesus Christ, and you can see part of the why of the Christian revival. Mao, though he did not plan it

EAST AND SOUTHEAST ASIA

 TOTALLY RESTRICTED
Mongolia(2.9 — .006)
North Korea (27.46 — .19)

 EXTREMELY RESTRICTED
Kampuchea (15.82 — .1)
Laos (5.73 — .11)
Vietnam (75.8 — 5.79)

 HIGHLY RESTRICTED
Burma (54.9 — 4.01)
China (1,127.3 — 1.5; but see pp. 42-43)
Malaysia (22.05 — 1.65)

 MODERATELY RESTRICTED
Brunei (.22 — .02)
Thailand (85.62 — .97)

 EMERGING RESTRICTIONS
Taiwan (24.67 — 2.49)

(In parentheses: **first,** estimated TOTAL population for the year 2000;
second, estimated CHRISTIAN population in the year 2000.)
All figures in MILLIONS

that way, did a good job of preparing the most populated nation in the world to receive the gospel of Jesus Christ.[15]

Communications improvements brought about under Communism in China have also helped the potential for rapid spread of Christianity. In 1949, there were 75,000 kilometers of serviceable roads in China; today there are over 890,000 kilometers of roads.

The potential for radio ministries has vastly increased, as more and more people have radios. In addition, one official lan-

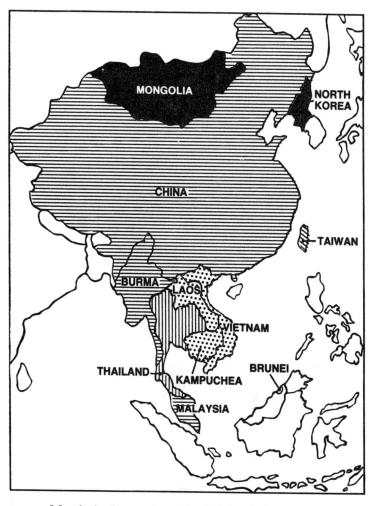

guage, Mandarin, has replaced the 300 "main languages" in use before the 1949 Revolution.

The situation in China appears to be an example of ways that missionary efforts can be assisted by the effects of Communism.

* * *

SOUTH AND SOUTHWEST ASIA

 EXTREMELY RESTRICTED
Afghanistan (36.65 — .016)
Bhutan (2.15 — .002)
Iran (66.59 — 46)
Iraq (24.45 — .71)
Kuwait (3.18 — .12)
North Yemen (13.75 — .005)
Qatar (.4 — .04)
Saudi Arabia (20.5 — .31)
South Yemen (3.43 — .002)
Syria (15.82 — 1.1)
Turkey (72.50 — ,19)

 HIGHLY RESTRICTED
Bahrain (.54 — .02)
Maldives (.2 — .0003)
Nepal (23.2 — .01)
Oman (1.64 — .007)

 MODERATELY RESTRICTED
Bangladesh (144.35 — 1.12)
India (1,059.43 — 49.79)
Israel (5.49 — .11)
Jordan (4.23 — .19)
Pakistan (146.92 — 2.91)
Seychelles (.1 — .09)
Sri Lanka (21.34 — 1.7)
United Arab Emirates (.7 — .03)

 EMERGING RESTRICTIONS
Lebanon (6.12 — 3.21)

(In parentheses: **first,** estimated TOTAL population for the year 2000;
second, estimated CHRISTIAN population in the year 2000.)
All figures in MILLIONS

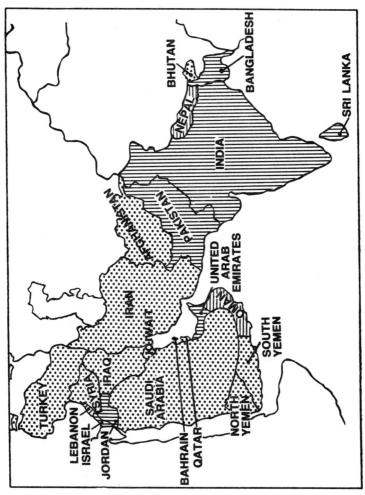

In China, India, the Muslim nations, and elsewhere around the globe, about 76 percent of the world's non-Christians now live in one of the approximately 17,000 unreached groups. Or, to put it another way, about 2.5 billion of the world's 3.3 billion non-Christians (as of 1985) live on the other side of a cultural barrier which 90 percent of the 249,000 foreign missionaries currently fielded by the developed world are not equipped to cross.

In attempting to reach the world's non-Christians, the importance of having specialized training to break through these cultural barriers cannot be overestimated.

Since the 1960s, the field of *intercultural communication* has been based on precisely this realization, as well as on the examples throughout history of the misunderstandings and even armed conflicts which have resulted when peoples from groups removed by space, ideology, appearance, and behavior try to interact.[16]

Though the focus of intercultural communication is largely secular, its findings have much relevance for missions work. When we cross these intercultural barriers in the name of Christ, we clearly need to have the skills to successfully share our deepest feelings and perceptions with members of groups vastly different from our own.

For the greatest chance of success, we must not only speak the other person's language, but also be fluent in his or her culture. For example, Gladys Alworth became so assimilated into Chinese society that the local church selected her for the position of "Bible woman," a role heretofore reserved for native Chinese women.

According to a pioneering model developed by L. E. Sarbaugh, several different factors will affect whether or not we are understood *and believed* as we witness about the Lord in a foreign culture. These factors are:

- Similarity of verbal and nonverbal communication systems. (Requirements include not only the same language, but similar kinds of gestures, touching behaviors, conversational distance, gaze behaviors, and clothing style.)

- Similarity of world view. (Are we optimistic? Do we believe that high effort leads to success? Many cultures wouldn't agree.)

- Similarity of intent and goals. (Are we perceived as having positive feelings towards the other person, and the same goals for the interchange?)
- Similarity of hierarchicalness. (Do we see each other as equals, rather than as a superior talking to a subordinate?)[17]

In short, to successfully communicate with (and evangelize) the roughly three-fourths of the world's non-Christians who are in the 17,000 unreached groups, we need good cross-cultural training.

OTHER TRENDS

In preparing for the changing contexts of the twenty-first-century mission, we need to understand the implication of a variety of additional data. Here is a summary of some of these statistics, taken from the *World Christian Encyclopedia:*

- On the positive side, the *number* of professing Christians in the world has grown substantially, from 558 million in 1900 to 1.4 billion by 1980. Though the unfinished task of the Great Commission is growing, the number of saved would appear to be growing as well.
- There are now "Christians and organized Christian churches in every inhabited country on earth," the encyclopedia claims. It should be noted, however, that "every inhabited country on earth" is by no means the same as "every tribe and language and people and nation" (Revelation 5:9). The difference is the 17,000 unreached people groups where three-fourths of the world's non-Christians now live.

LATIN AMERICA

 EXTREMELY RESTRICTED
Cuba (15.26 — 5.3)

 MODERATELY RESTRICTED
Guyana (1.25 — .6)
Nicaragua (5.15 — 5.12)
Suriname (.9 — .68)

 EMERGING RESTRICTIONS
Chile (15.36 — 13.92)
Colombia (51.46 — 49.63)
Costa Rica (3.70 — 3.54)
Mexico (132.24 — 125.59)
Panama (3.23 — 2.9)

(In parentheses: **first,** estimated TOTAL population for the year 2000;
second, estimated CHRISTIAN population in the year 2000.)
All figures in MILLIONS

- In two-thirds of the world's 223 countries,
  Christians now form more than 50 percent of the
  population. "This spread is uneven, though,"
  Barrett says. "Christians number over 90 percent
  in 100 countries, less than 10 percent in 51
  countries, less than 1 percent in 24 countries, and
  less than 0.1 percent in six countries: Afghanistan,
  Bhutan, Nepal, Somalia, North Yemen, and South
  Yemen."

- Since 1900, "Christianity has become massively
  accepted as the religion of the . . . Third World,
  Africa in particular," according to Barrett. The
  number of Christians in the world's less developed
  countries has increased from 83 million in 1900 to
  643 million by 1980. By mid-1985, an estimated

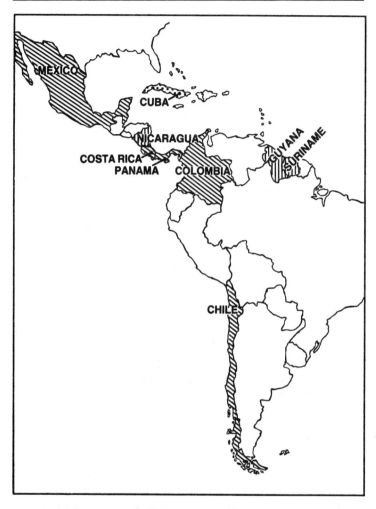

44.3 percent of all Christians lived in the Third World. This is expected to increase to 48.7 percent by the year 2000.

• Disturbingly, 190 million Christians—or 13.3 percent of all Christians—live in absolute poverty. "Half of them live in Latin America, a third in Africa, the rest in South and Southeast Asia." Put differently, 24 percent of the world's 780 million "absolutely poor" are Christians. This, as Barrett says, makes Christianity "the religion of the poor."

- In 1900, the world's "largest Christian culture was that of the Russians; by 1930 it had been smashed."
- Also in 1900, 83 percent of the world's Christians were Western—50 percent in Europe, 19 percent in Russia, and 14 percent in North America. By the year 2000, however, it's expected that "Latin America will have 28 percent of the world's Christians, followed by Europe with 21 percent, Africa and Asia each with 19 percent, and North America with 13 percent."
- "Since 1970, the largest Christian language has been Spanish, with 207 million church-member native speakers in 1980."[18]
- Finally, a statistic from the January 1984 issue of *Theology Today:* "Western churches are losing adherents at the rate of 7,600 members per day. African churches are gaining members at the rate of 16,400 per day, roughly 12,000 through the birth rate and the rest through conversions."[19]

In summary, the world at the conclusion of the twentieth century is vastly different in terms of our mission context than the world just a century before. As we have attempted to live up to the optimistic projections of nineteenth-century strategists, we have been thwarted by a number of factors, including massive population increases, major population shifts, Communist revolutions, underestimated cultural barriers, and a decline in the growth rate of the missionary force.

Our advantage, hopefully, is an increased level of humility as we understand how enormous is the challenge before us and how much we require the Lord's guidance and support so His Great Commission might be pursued more effectively.

If we fail to become more effective, the victims will be people—billions of them, in fact.

Therefore we turn to the Lord with prayers that He will guide His people in this work, as we resolve to do more in the great unfinished task.

QUESTIONS FOR THOUGHT AND REVIEW

- What's gone wrong with global evangelism?
- What obstacles need to be surmounted to get the mission of the Church back on track?
- Without reading further in the book, what special knowledge and sensitivities do you think a New Envoy would require?

Documentation and Notes

1. Barrett, *World Christian Encyclopedia*, p. 4. This 3.3 billion estimate for the world's non-Christian population is computed from figures supplied by Barrett (published 1982) which provide a global estimate of 3.233 non-Christians as of mid-1985. I have increased this number slightly to 3.3 billion, based on the more recent world population estimates provided in the *1985 World Population Data Sheet* (Washington, D.C.: Population Reference Bureau, April 1985).

2. For consistency, I use the 6.2 billion projection for the year 2000 quoted in Barrett, *World Christian Encyclopedia*, p. 4, compared to the 6.1 billion projection on the *1985 World Population Data Sheet*, from which also the 7.8 billion figure is taken.

3. Barrett, p. 4, and *1985 World Population Data Sheet*.

4. Sources for the information contained in the maps and charts in this chapter include Freedom House, Keston College, The Research Center for Religion and Human Rights in Closed Societies, the *World Christian Encyclopedia*, and ISSACHAR field and survey work.

The list of restrictive countries was prepared by ISSACHAR Frontier Missions Research. Background criteria for the list ranged from international political rights and civil liberties, to issues such as the number of missionaries sent and received, and the nature and availability of missionary visas. Virtually all the figures and statistics utilized in compiling the list are from 1975-86.

To the ISSACHAR list I added population data compiled from *World Christian Encyclopedia,* pp. 133-771. These are projections, of course, and subject to dispute, but I think they will provide the reader with a general sense of the numbers involved.

5. A more comprehensive report on National Religious Freedom and Accessibility is now being prepared, and is due to be released by ISSACHAR in 1987.

6. *Freedom in the World* (New York: Freedom House).

7. Ralph Winter, *Mission Frontiers,* August/September 1985, p. 3.

8. Winter, p. 3.

9. Winter, p. 3.

10. Sharon E. Mumper, "New Strategies to Evangelize Muslims Gain Effectiveness," in *Christianity Today,* May 17, 1985, p. 75.

11. J. Christy Wilson Jr., quoted in *Christianity Today,* "New Strategies to Evangelize Muslims Gain Effectiveness," May 17, 1985, p. 75.

12. Barrett, p. 231.

13. Barrett, in telephone interview with the author, November 11, 1986. Barrett's most recent figures on Christianity in China are to be published in the "Annual Statistical Table of Global Mission 1987" in the *International Bulletin of Missionary Research,* January 1987.

14. Barrett, in telephone interview with the author, November 11, 1986.

15. Carl Lawrence, *The Church in China* (Minneapolis: Bethany House Publishers, 1985), p. 142.

16. Larry A. Samovar and Richard E. Porter, *Intercultural Communication: A Reader* (Belmont, California: Wadsworth Publishing Company, 1976), p. 4. For more examples, see Leederer and Burdick's *The Ugly American,* the pioneering work in this field.

17. L. E. Sarbaugh, "A Systematic Framework for Analyzing Intercultural Communication," in *International and Intercultural Communication Annual,* vol. V, December 1979.

18. Barrett, pp. 3-9, 11, and 24.

19. John Mulder, quoted in *The National Christian Reporter,* July 20, 1984, p. 2.

INTRODUCING . . . GOD'S NEW ENVOYS

SO far we have explored (1) the mandate for the global mission, (2) why the unfinished task of the Great Commission is actually further from completion than ever before, and (3) the new context facing our missions outreach in the century ahead.

We have thus identified the needs, the problems, and the opportunities. Now, the beginnings of a solution—God's New Envoys.

THEIR PLACE IN THE MISSION FIELD

In this and the next few chapters, we'll be developing the concept of God's New Envoys and discussing how they are to be selected and trained. First, however, it might be helpful to look at the New Envoys in context, to see where they fit in the overall fabric of the global missions effort.

To begin with, it must be understood that these New Envoys are intended to *supplement* the efforts of traditional missionaries—and not to replace them or to diminish the resources which support them. In fact, I believe that to fulfill their portion of the twenty-first-century missions mandate, traditional missionaries will require an increased allocation of resources and will need to be fielded in larger numbers than before.

I also think we will find it productive to refine and intensify the training of traditional missionaries. They will need stronger specialized skills to meet the considerable challenge of more effectively evangelizing non-Christians in the countries still open to traditional missionary approaches.

Later we'll explore a new model for evaluating which people groups are best served by traditional missionaries and which are more effectively reached by the New Envoys. We'll also clarify the distinctions between traditional missionaries and the New Envoys in the areas of training, support modalities, and operating styles. For the present, however, a generalized comparison of the three basic groups of "full-time soul-winners" might be of help, along with a look at this new group—God's New Envoys.

Within these four groups—representing several million Christians throughout the world—resides the entirety of the human force now at work to activate the world's nominal Christians and to bring to Christ the 3.3 billion who are not Christians at all. The chart on pages 58-59 gives a general description of each group, beginning with the smallest and working up to the largest.

As the chart shows, God's New Envoys are envisioned as both the newest and the smallest segment of the large group of Christians now devoting some or all of their lives to evangelization. Notwithstanding their relatively small numbers, however, the New Envoys have been given a disproportionately large mandate: to reach the growing number of non-Christians who are currently out of reach of traditional missionary efforts.

Also it should be understood that although God's New Envoys will be "tentmakers" as the term is popularly understood in Christian missions, they will be *more* than tentmakers. "Tentmaking" refers primarily to an economic factor: a missionary's being financially self-supported. But God's New Envoys will be distinguished from traditional missionaries by much more than financial self-support, especially in terms of training and function and target mission. They will be *specialists* in every sense of the word.

THE SPECIAL CHALLENGES THEY MUST MEET

To meet the urgent needs in contemporary missions and to accelerate the global missions effort, these special new workers in God's vineyard will need to be very special indeed. In the words which have inspired missionary efforts for centuries,

> The harvest truly is great, but the labourers are few: pray
> ye therefore the Lord of the harvest, that he would send
> forth labourers into his harvest. (Luke 10:2, KJV)

We have prayed to the Lord of the harvest, and we will continue to pray. It is hoped the New Envoys will be a portion of the answer. If so, they will be what Paul describes as "Christ's ambassadors" (2 Corinthians 5:20), meaning the messengers of the gospel of reconciliation—reconciling men and women of *all* races, *all* tribes, *all* language groups, and *all* nations to God in Christ. As an urgently needed new breed of cross-cultural workers, God's New Envoys will be able to function as His messengers of reconciliation in countries and among people groups where pure evangelists and traditional missionaries may not.

Working within their special domain of closed countries and closed groups, these New Envoys will strive to make disciples, to disciple the nations, and, especially, to reach the world's unreached—beginning now, and throughout the twenty-first century.

In contrast to the church growth movement's strategy of "winning the winnable," the New Envoys will take for their harvesting target the groups that often have proved the least winnable—yielding the greatest dangers, the most frustrations, and the lowest conversion rates.

THE CHURCH'S WORLDWIDE EVANGELISTIC WORK FORCE—FOUR GROUPS

1. GOD'S NEW ENVOYS
(For the most part, these will be independently operating, self-supporting, and cross-trained in a nonmissions area. In most cases New Envoys will need to be silent about their "missionary vocation.")

Their mandate: To work in countries closed to traditional approaches and win the "hard-to-win" to Christ.

Their training and strategic approach: Largely new.

Current strength: A few hundred (and these are not yet called New Envoys.)

Minimum number required: 100,000. Though this number may at first sound high, I see it as a bare minimum to accomplish the job that needs to be done. When you consider that in the United States alone there are currently 385,000 places of regular worship (a vast majority of them Christian churches), it is not hard to imagine that the United States could produce 50,000 Envoys, with an additional 50,000 coming from Christian churches in other parts of the world.[1]

2. TRADITIONAL MISSIONARIES
(These tend to be under centralized control, to be supported by others, and to have most of their training in traditional missions areas. They usually can be open about their missionary calling.)

Their mandate: To evangelize winnable populations or people groups within "open" countries.

Their training and strategic approach: Traditional, but being upgraded.

Current strength: About 249,000, of whom about 32,500 (a figure which is growing rapidly) are sent out by Third World churches.[2]

Number currently required: About 300,000.

3. OTHER FULL-TIME CHRISTIAN WORKERS
(This group includes pastors and other full-time ministers who are actively involved in evangelization. Its members are supported by others and almost always operate under some form of authority—a church committee, governing board, bishop, etc. The nature of their ministry is almost always openly disclosed.

Their mandate: To activate nominal Christians, to support the further growth of those who are already involved, and to "evangelize" (often nominal Christians) within their own geographic or ecclesiastical areas.

Their primary target: In many cases, the 1.5 billion who already are professing Christians.

Current strength: About three million worldwide.[3]

Number currently required: Difficult to estimate. Depends on laity's willingness to shoulder more of the burden of evangelism.

4. EVANGELIZING CHRISTIAN LAITY
(A voluntary group. Self-supporting, nonregimented, with widely divergent levels of training and willingness to assist in furtherance of the Great Commission.)

Their mandate: Interpreted differently by different denominations.

Their target: Whatever population each group member selects for evangelization.

Their training and strategic approach: Varies widely.

Current strength: Difficult to measure.

Number currently required: Many millions more.

THEIR BASIC QUALIFICATIONS

Like any other missionary, the New Envoys must be wholeheartedly devoted to Christ and His mission on earth, believing in the availability of salvation only in and through Jesus Christ. Also, like any other missionary, God's New Envoys must be physically sound, emotionally stable, socially aware, culturally sensitive, biblically literate, and very strong in their prayer lives.

In addition, they will need to be equipped with special strategies. To achieve their challenging mandate in the face of major changes in the twenty-first-century mission field, they will require additional and very special qualifications, as shown in the following chart.

GOD'S NEW ENVOYS—QUALIFICATIONS

To be truly effective, God's New Envoys must be:

(1) Physically, emotionally, and spiritually self-reliant—to a very high degree.

(2) Adaptable.

(3) Alert to the emerging missions context.

(4) Cross-disciplinary trained.

(5) Equipped with broad new strategic thinking.

(6) Prepared with special strategies for responding to opportunities presented by need.

SELECTION

TRAINING

STRATEGIES

These qualifications, as indicated, can be condensed into three separate, yet interrelated categories: selection criteria, training, and strategies. We will look at these more closely in the coming chapters—sources and training requirements, the foundations for broad strategic approaches, and more specialized tactics to maximize the effectiveness of New Envoys whose work is conducted in situations of high physical need.

There will be much here that is new, and hopefully some thoughts that may be adapted to increase the effectiveness of traditional missionaries and ministries at home as well.

Together these concepts form the key to finding and preparing God's New Envoys.

When mastered, they will also be the key to their success.

QUESTIONS FOR THOUGHT AND REVIEW

- Explain the position of New Envoys with respect to traditional missionaries, pastors, and other full-time workers.
- Using your own words, make a list of criteria for selecting New Envoys.

Documentation and Notes

1. David Barrett, *World Christian Encyclopedia*, p. 725.
2. Barrett, p. 17.
3. Barrett, p. 17, cites a 1980 figure of 3,199,000 "full-time Christian personnel, nationals plus aliens."

SELECTING A MISSIONS ELITE

GOD'S New Envoys must be called from diverse sources. The areas where we seek them should include the developing world as well as the First World. In fact, a Third World background may well increase their credibility within many target groups.

SOURCES FOR NEW ENVOYS

These are the categories of people who are the sources for New Envoys:

1. *Pre-career people,* either with ministerial/missionary training already or at least the inclination to be so trained.

2. *Mid-career people,* with ministerial/missionary training or at least the inclination to be so trained.

3. *Post-career people,* preferably with ministerial/missionary training or at least the inclination to be so trained.

Clearly, good prospects to become New Envoys can be found within a wide variety of identity groups. They may be found among current college students, on both the undergraduate and graduate levels—majoring in subject areas such as comparative religion, biblical studies, science, agriculture, animal husbandry, engineering, medicine, anthropology, sociology, teaching, international law, diplomacy, intercultural communications, and international business.

Executives and professionals of all kinds are potential prospects for New Envoy training. So are pastors and missionaries on furlough seeking a new challenge in their careers. Men and women in the military, teachers, and people working in diplomatic posts already have performed as New Envoys in closed countries.

For some mid-career traditional missionaries, the role of the New Envoy may be exactly the fresh challenge they're looking for. Remember, however, that the working environment for the New Envoy can be quite different from that for traditional missionaries. Even more importantly, the low-key, often covert, and one-on-one discipling style required of the New Envoy may prove frustrating to the traditional missionary, especially if he or she is accustomed to high levels of harvesting for the Lord.

In a similar vein, it must be stressed that the skills of a successful pastor or a successful traditional missionary are very special—and a glorious gift from God—and may not fit comfortably into the less flamboyant, though often more entrepreneurial evangelism style the New Envoy must employ.

Some current missionaries and evangelizing development workers already are functioning as New Envoys, in every aspect except for the title. As valuable as their individual contributions might be, however, this role switching within Christ's current army is not the intent of this book.

Rather, I believe we must use the banner of God's New Envoys to raise up a *new* army—mobilizing thousands of previously underutilized Christians, providing them their own challenging and rewarding opportunity for a lifetime of service to the Lord.

One would hope that this cause might be persuasive enough to reach some of those who previously have held back from personal evangelism. Some of this group have mistakenly assumed it is wrong to attempt to change another's religion. If so, they themselves are wrong on two counts: first, because it is actually the height of righteousness to share one's most valuable possession—the knowledge of the Lord; second, because no man can change another's religion. The true conversion must always be conducted by the Lord Himself.

Others who have resisted the call to take part in personal evangelism have done so because of the mistaken assumption that "all religions are equally good and equally loved by God" or perhaps some notion that the "true path" would involve some sort of harmonious and mutually tolerant mixture of all the religions in the world.

For a refutation of these two false positions—known technically as relativism and syncretism—one needs merely to take a more careful look at Scripture.

Or, if one prefers, one might look at some of the "fruits" of the other religions (such as Islam) and quasi-religions (such as Communism) which flourish when the cause of Christ is not adequately championed.[1]

One reason we might hope for many to respond to the call to join the ranks of God's New Envoys is a response to the longing which is innate, though not always recognized, in us all: the longing for reconciliation and closeness with God, a need that can be satisfied in part through devotion of greater portions of one's time and talent to His service. For some, this longing will be experienced as "not being right with God." For others, it may be perceived as what might be called an "unmet altruistic imperative." By that I mean the inner conflicts resulting from a present inability to fulfill one's sense of a calling to do good in service to others.

One possible source for New Envoy candidates might be from among those who are frustrated at our apparent helplessness in bringing peace to this world. Christians among the highly motivated men and women who serve in the Peace Corps will appreciate opportunities to work for peace through the

one-on-one contact that comes through serving as a New Envoy.
Christians who have completed their military obligation will
also be sensitive to the important role New Envoys can play in
bringing lasting peace.

As incidents of public and private terrorism multiply and
the potential for nuclear annihilation expands, the more attrac
tive will be the prospect of making a lasting contribution as a
New Envoy to a better, more peaceful world.

Increasingly, the world's unreached peoples find themselves captivated by "religions" of violence. Within one group,
the violence is practiced against women (in forms of Islam and
animism). Within another, nonbelievers must die (in Islamic
"Holy Wars"). In a third, the potential victims are the whole
world (in Communism's quest for world domination).

People in these unreached groups are also the victims of
Western materialism, which has robbed them of resources that
should be theirs. And we're all potential victims of nuclear proliferation, which diverts resources from humane endeavors and
threatens to exterminate us all.

It would be an exaggeration, of course, to say the New Envoys can bring an end to all this violence. Most assuredly, only
the Lord Jesus has that power. But those who become Envoys
will know they are standing up against that violence in a highly
moral and caring way, and that each new individual they help
bring to Christ will increase the total of our fellow human beings
who can live in an eternal paradise of peace.

Being a New Envoy should also appeal to those who want
a firsthand experience within another culture. It is also an ideal
way to share profoundly close and profoundly satisfying human
fellowship across cultural lines.

In short, it is an excellent vocation for Christians who
care, who want to learn, and who want to do more to spread the
kingdom of God.

SELECTION CRITERIA

The most basic criteria for selecting New Envoys are that they want to serve and that they seem to have the capacity for service under the particular circumstances of restriction, aloneness, and potential danger. With so many available avenues for service to the Lord, it is important that God's New Envoys be people who are best suited to this task.

One essential component for the Envoys, in my opinion, is a sense of wonder: a genuine desire to be immersed in a complex foreign culture and to learn as much as possible about how it works. This sense of wonder is not dissimilar to the thought expressed in Paul's prayer for comprehension in Ephesians 3:

> And I pray that you, being rooted and established in love,
> may have power, together with all the saints, to grasp how
> wide and long and high and deep is the love of Christ, and
> to know this love that surpasses knowledge—that you
> may be filled to the measure of all the fullness of God.
> (Ephesians 3:17-19)

Granted, as we study a foreign culture we are not directly studying God; but in a sense we are. For can we not learn of the Father by learning about His children, whom He created and loves so much?

With a true willingness to learn, the Envoys' days will be filled with new knowledge, and they will be more trusted by the people they seek to evangelize.

The New Envoy also must have or develop the capacity to see "foreigners" as God does. Borrowing from Gordon Aeschliman and Sam Wilson's colorful expression, the New Envoy must be able to understand that

> "God loves a Muslim as much as he does Billy Graham.
> We have to let go of prejudices and fears and see *all* people
> as precious."[2]

Elsewhere, Aeschliman echoes a similar theme in an article on missions to the Soviet Union:

> "But what about when we do recognize evil in their
> society? God requires us to respond by seeking ways to
> love them. . . . We must learn to love the Russians with
> the same tenderness that Jesus has for us, and that he has
> for the Russians."[3]

Another side of this ability to love—or possibly its result—is a willingness to go to corrupt countries, to dirty countries, even to sinful countries. The New Envoy must have the sincere willingness to go wherever necessary and to do whatever is required to bring the unreached to Christ.

Obviously this kind of service demands that the Envoy be more than usually healthy and physically resilient. The kind of physical constitution which requires frequent medical tune-ups would be a great handicap in most unreached areas, where medical assistance is often days away.

In one of my recent visits to our field staff in East Africa, I joked with a veteran missionary that driving skills on ravaged roads should be taught in all missions schools. We both laughed, but I'm not sure I was wrong. Perhaps one can learn the driving skills in-country, but one should certainly arrive there with a body resilient enough to take the strain.

Also on the subject of missionaries and strain, conventional wisdom in missionary selection would seem to indicate that there is less wear and tear on missionaries in isolated regions if the missionary is accompanied by a spouse. In the case of New Envoys, I'm not sure that having a spouse is always required, or is even desirable in some situations. To begin with, there's an element of physical danger in some of the more completely closed areas. In such cases, as under a severe Communist regime, I suspect that single Envoys might feel less vulnerable than those who had an in-country spouse who was also liable to arrest.

Individual situations vary, but there are also many cross-cultural situations where a lone Envoy would become acculturated faster than one buffered by a spouse and maybe children as well. The point is, there are no simple rules. Certainly an unmarried Envoy should not resist going into an otherwise appropriate missions area simply for lack of a spouse.

Adaptability is another requisite for New Envoys. They must be able to make the most of whatever opportunities the Lord brings them. Likewise, they must be flexible enough to let go of situations which are not turning out. In such cases, if people will not welcome them and listen to their words, they must be prepared to "shake the dust off their feet" and move on (Matthew 10:14).

Like the desert fathers of the fourth century, the New Envoys must be people who have cultivated great patience. To prevail, especially in some of the more bureaucratic and restrictive regimes, they will often have to sit and listen and wait.

Similarly, they must be able to find satisfaction in small results. Many times they will have to make do with a tiny mustard seed of a conversion and with a delayed flowering of their efforts which may never be visible to them at all.

They must always be humble enough to remember that though they are the ones who plant and water, "only God . . . makes things grow" (1 Corinthians 3:7).

The New Envoy will also need to be proficient at a ministry of igniting others. He or she must be a teacher, an inspirer, a model for others. New Envoys must demonstrate their beliefs through their own example. They must be able to work through the local structure and empower those who will be left behind, after they leave.

Ray Giles, now co-director of personnel for the Christian Missionary Fellowship, has had a fifteen-year missionary career in some especially difficult fields, most recently in a capacity in which he could easily qualify as one of God's New Envoys. In a recent article, Ray outlined three important indicators of eventual success in difficult missions fields, as suggested by his research:

> The most significant factor is one's relationship to Jesus Christ. . . . A missionary must be content with his or her position in Jesus Christ and be able to sustain that relationship through prayer and meditation on the Word without the usual props and promptings of the church.

> Second . . . is a healthy self-esteem. By that I mean one that does not run roughshod over colleagues or demand center stage. Even more dangerous is a low self-esteem, because there is little on the field to boost self- esteem.

> A third factor has to do with mood swings, especially those that shift to depression frequently. Successful candidates [the research indicates] . . . were rated by their acquaintances as rarely experiencing moodiness.[4]

THE THREE PILLARS OF SPIRITUAL SUPPORT

Building on Ray's observations—which I heartily endorse—I think a little more needs to be said about the New Envoys' basis of spiritual strength. Especially important are three pillars of support: the Lord's presence, Scripture, and unity with other believers.

Even in sometimes desperately lonely places, the Envoys will never be alone. They will be aided in all their trials by the constraining love of Christ and by the Great Comforter, the Holy Spirit.

Not having "the usual props and promptings of the church," however, they will probably need to turn to Scripture with greater regularity, certainly on a daily basis. Scripture will also be the common philosophical basis for all the Envoys, ensuring that they are "thoroughly equipped for every good work" (2 Timothy 3:17).

Along with the love of Christ, Scripture will be the transcendent commonality which empowers New Envoys to work together as one—though separated by enormous distances, being without central leadership, and coming from diverse backgrounds—to achieve the overarching goal of the Great Commission.

An additional important selection criterion for New Envoys is their ability to work in harmony as members of diverse groups of committed Christians, where differences in background and training will produce differences in doctrine and approach.

In part, this unity of the New Envoys will be achieved automatically by the severity of the missions field. This will be attested by most anyone who has experienced missions efforts in some of the extremely restricted nations where New Envoys will be called to work. In part, this ability to work together must be taught.

Don Hamilton, director of TMQ Research, recently conducted a survey of 349 tentmaker missionaries working overseas. The responses of the 16 percent of those surveyed who were found to be most effective in the field were then analyzed and some common characteristics identified.

Here are five of the characteristics identified by the Hamilton Survey, along with Don's comments about them. All five, in my opinion, will also prove to be important indicators of the effectiveness of God's New Envoys.

1. *They had led an evangelistic Bible study before going overseas.*

   It is felt that this is significant because conventional witnessing methods, such as door-to-door visitation, passing out tracts, holding street meetings, etc. are not wise or even possible in many places in the world. Building relationships, earning the right to be heard are key. An evangelistic Bible study is a fine strategy.

2. *Their main reason for going was to share the Gospel of Christ.*

> Travel, money, desire to be independent were not strong motivating factors. Without motivation to share the Gospel, less effective tentmakers quickly burn out in the often hostile environments.

3. *They believed God called them to be tentmakers.*

> When the going got tough, many indicated it was their deep conviction of God's calling that carried them through. The emphasis was on absolute assurance that this is where God wanted them.

4. *They had experience in actively sharing their faith at home.*

> Their expression was that "If you hadn't done it here, you wouldn't there, where it is 100 times tougher." As compared to the "average" tentmaker, twice as many of these highly effective tentmakers witnessed about Christ overseas, and three times as many led others to Christ while there.

5. *They had strong relationships with their home local church.*

> Their attendance and participation was consistent, and their church considered their tentmaking work true missions activity. Most were commissioned by their church, and reported back to and felt accountable to their church.[5]

Now, having discussed the selection processes for the New Envoys, the next subject is their training.

QUESTIONS FOR THOUGHT AND REVIEW

- Explain where potential New Envoys are to be found.
- Describe what is so new and different about them.
- Discuss your reactions to the three factors suggested by Ray Giles and the findings of Don Hamilton's tentmaker effectiveness survey. How relevant do you think these factors are to the effectiveness of New Envoys?

Documentation and Notes

1. To further explore the impacts of syncretism and relativism, see the articles by Peter Beyerhaus and Donald McGavran on these subjects in *Christopaganism or Indigenous Christianity?* (South Pasadena, Calif.: William Carey Library, 1975).

2. Wilson and Aeschliman, *The Hidden Half,* quoted in *Mission Frontiers,* August/September 1985, p. 17.

3. Gordon Aeschliman, "Anyone Love a Russian?" in *World Christian,* January/February 1985, p. 6.

4. Ray A. Giles, "To Fulfill the Task," in *Unto the Uttermost* by Doug Priest Jr. (Pasadena: William Carey Library, 1984), p. 303.

5. "Summary of Report #1" taken from *The Hamilton Tentmaker Survey* published by TMQ Research (Don Hamilton, Director), 312 Melcanyon Road, Duarte, California 91010.

TRAINING FOR THE CHALLENGE

IN designing a training program for God's New Envoys, we need to create a curriculum for a group which has not yet been assembled, the goal of which is to do something which has rarely before been done. And I'd like to suggest even more hurdles that must be cleared.

First, this training needs to be very widely available. It should attract both college and graduate students from all over the Christian world, and yet also appeal to more mature candidates who already are in mid-career, offering them training—or retraining—that provides the least possible interruption of their current careers and their lives.

Second, this training needs to be interesting and challenging enough so that bright, resourceful, and well-educated people will be attracted. Our goal is to attract people who are already successful—whether in a school setting or in a fruitful career. The mission of God's New Envoys is difficult and demanding. Only superior candidates need apply.

Third, this training needs to be built on an unquestionably sound biblical base, so that candidates from the broadest possible range of Christian denominations will be comfortable with it. As stated earlier, the New Envoys are seen as a bridge to span the rifts caused by denominational rivalries. Nothing less than a unified Body working together can achieve the Great Commission; nor, as Christians, should we *accept* anything less than a truly united attempt.

THE EMERGING CONTEXT

Earlier we described the "emerging missions context" of the twenty-first century. Naturally, in order for New Envoy training to be relevant, it must include instruction that will enable Envoys to evangelize effectively in the midst of these new environments. Depending on the country or people group where they will be working, they must be prepared to face any or all of the following nine elements:

1. The exploding non-Christian population.
2. The increasing inaccessibility of people groups that need to hear the gospel.
3. The problems of reaching across cultural barriers and being believed, trusted, and understood.
4. The shift of the Church's population centrum from the developed West to the Third World.
5. The growing willingness (and demands) of Third World Christians to have a substantial role in the missions effort.
6. The need for church planting strategies to fit countries where Christians may receive no outside support.
7. The shift of the Church's membership base from the church of the haves to "the church of the poor."
8. The high incidence of physical need within unreached people groups.
9. The ambition of the leadership of many of these unreached groups to "catch up" with the prosperity and power of the developed world at an accelerating rate.

From a review of these nine aspects of the emerging missions context, we can develop specific performance objectives for New Envoy training. These are not intended to indicate *all* the things a New Envoy should know related to the emerging missions context, but they will suggest some of the kinds of knowledge to be required.

Following their training, New Envoys should be able to:

1. List and explain the strategies for reaching (that is, evangelizing and converting) within people groups where there is a high level of need.

2. Identify the techniques for entering people groups normally considered "closed."

3. Explain and demonstrate techniques for communicating successfully with people from a different culture—paying special attention to dissimilar values, ethnocentricity, nonverbal communication (such as proxemics and gaze behaviors), and the culturally value-laden conversion issues such as polygamy or alcohol consumption.

4. Demonstrate a sound knowledge of the Third World— its strengths as well as its weaknesses. Describe the more common Third World social systems and hierarchical structures. Explain the rationale for working "under" Third World nationals.

5. Describe five or more church-planting strategies designed for countries where traditional churches are not tolerated. Explain and differentiate the techniques for discipling, "friendship evangelization," "relationship evangelization," and building up self-replicating Christ groups.

6. Explain basic techniques for winning another person to Christ, especially when that person is a member of a cultural group different from your own. Be able to demonstrate these techniques in practice. Also, demonstrate actual experience utilizing these techniques with various ethnic groups under controlled, supervised circumstances where your approach can be critiqued and improved.

7. Explain and demonstrate in actual practice techniques for organizing and perpetuating a Christ group. Participate in this group both as leader and member.

8. Explain techniques for teaching local nationals to take up the missionary task, working independently of you, without any outside support.

9. Develop and explain a personally comfortable rationale for operating as a "covert" missionary.

10. Demonstrate acceptable mastery of whatever language will be required in your missions field. (*Note:* Depending on the situation, some of this mastery might have to be acquired after entering the missions field.)

11. List and explain the basic tenets of the dominant religions and quasi-religions (such as Communism) within your selected missions field. List ten strengths of this religion; and list ten ways in which Christianity might better meet the local population's needs.

At all phases of their training, it is vital that the Envoys learn attitudes that are culturally nonjudgmental. They must be taught that they are not going abroad to make the world *American* Christians or *Japanese* Christians or *French* Christians or *Belgian* Christians. Rather, they must strive to bring unreached peoples to faith and obedience in Christ, so these peoples can then be Christians in a way that is both biblically sound and authentic within their indigenous cultural systems.

It is also imperative that all training place a high priority on quality—quality of preparation, quality of personal example, and quality of sharing with those whom you seek to bring to faith and obedience in Christ.

The expectation of the New Envoys is not that they will immediately—if ever—be able to lead large numbers of people to Christ, and certainly not in a brief period of time. It is assumed that in the areas where New Envoys will work, the conversion process will take a great deal of time, discretion, and skill.

Some, if not many, of the unreached groups where Envoys will work have already been evangelized, at least to a degree. The problem is that this evangelization has not "taken." The population or their government is just too resistive, and no indigenous churches have sprung up.

The solution to this resistiveness requires Envoys who will set a truly inspiring example of Christian conduct, and who must be equipped with the special skill of teaching disciples who can teach other disciples, who will then together be able to create an indigenous church.

God's New Envoys need to be effective one-on-one teachers. They must have the skills to'raise up disciples who can work independently as persuasive witnesses for Christ. We need look no further than the apostle Paul to understand the critical importance of a single convert who has the credentials to be persuasive to those within his own culture, and who has been properly inspired and taught.

The special mission of the New Envoy is one in which the greatest successes will probably be achieved by those whom the Envoy disciples, not by the Envoy himself.

SPECIAL DISCIPLINES

Obviously, each Envoy's training will vary, depending on where he or she goes to seek that training, and the degree to which such training takes place in the classroom or is acquired on the job or through independent study. In any case, the following will provide a general outline for the components and the disciplines which the Envoys' training should include:

1. *Biblical/theological studies*. Includes at least a year of scriptural studies and Christian apologetics to thoroughly prepare the Envoy to use the Bible as a tool—both for evangelization and for daily guidance and sustenance for himself.

2. *Cross-cultural training*. Includes language learning, traditional religions, cultural adjustment, issues in cross-cultural communication, social structure (authority patterns), cross-cultural exposure, and so on.

3. *Missiology.* Includes history of mission, theory of

mission, church growth case studies, theory and practice of symbiotic ministries, and so on.

4. *Development issues and global awareness*. Includes issues related to the relief-recovery-development continuum; economic, social, and political considerations affecting developing nations; world hunger and the politics of hunger; and so on.

5. *Spiritual growth*. Includes spiritual development prior to the beginning of the New Envoy's ministry and also spiritual training to keep that ministry Christ-centered and Spirit-filled.

6. *Passport skills*. Includes specialization in an area such as these: agriculture, education, suitable technology, health, nutrition, management, or internship with an international development agency.

If the prospective New Envoy is still in a formal academic environment and can afford the time, a variety of disciplines might prove highly fruitful as background for the New Envoy training: cultural anthropology, applied anthropology, comparative religion, sociology (with respect to group dynamics), world history, intercultural communication, world religions, studies of Communist systems and ideology (if applicable), and areas of engineering and agroscience that would enable the New Envoy to develop skills useful in a Third World setting.

It is assumed that the New Envoys' training will include both formal and nonformal education. Typically the formal education will be part of a degree program and will be credential-based. It will tend to be more preparatory in nature and require full-time learning. It will take place in an institution, with a teacher and preestablished standards of performance.

The nonformal portion of the education, on the other hand, will be more short-term and specific. It will take place part-time. It will be more practical and will more likely be customized to the specific needs of the Envoy in the specific situations he or she expects to meet. This nonformal education will probably take place in the community, possibly within a setting where the Envoy is receiving practice in some of the skills required in the field (for example: working in an ethnic ministry in an urban setting).

Quite possibly the Envoy will establish the performance criteria for this nonformal education and will be responsible for determining at what point the education has been a "success."

If the Envoy is to work in a context of need, additional areas of training also will be required. The amount of time spent on these areas will, of course, depend on the specific kinds of work the Envoy will undertake in the target group. For Envoys concerned with development and human need, the following areas are recommended:

- Principles of relief and development
- Project management techniques
- Theory and methods of mental and physical growth
- Public health techniques

A number of Christian relief and development organizations, such as Food for the Hungry, offer well-supervised field internship programs that could provide a prospective New Envoy with outstanding experience both in relief and development work and in Christian witness within a closed country. In many cases, these programs do not require extensive prior experience. There are three main criteria for acceptance: (1) a desire to serve in a Third World setting in Christ's name, (2) a willingness to learn the necessary relief and development skills, and (3) the ability to make a commitment of two to three years to this work.

By now it should be apparent that embedded within the New Envoy training are many of the basic components of traditional missionary instruction. Time permitting, it would certainly not be inappropriate for the New Envoy to complete all the traditional missionary basic training, in addition to the special skills required in the New Envoy context.

Practically, what this means is that a traditional missionary may well be attracted by the New Envoy field and seek to

acquire the New Envoy training at mid-career. Traditional missionaries who already have solid experience in some of the more
restrictive mission fields would be ideal candidates to become
New Envoys, and might find that the change would add new
challenge and enrichment to their vocations.

In addition, the Envoys should also have training in ways
to maintain their physical and psychological health, and a clear
understanding of the extreme physical, psychological, and
spiritual pressures they may experience.

Before they travel to their missions field, it is highly desirable that the New Envoys have already demonstrated strong
evangelization skills.

One excellent and productive way to hone these skills
might be in a ministry to foreign students in the educational institution where Envoys gain some of their training. This means
of evangelism training has special benefits, in addition to the
conversions achieved: It gives the Envoy candidate experience
working with a foreign population; and, because of the selection
process by which usually only the elite may study abroad, the
Envoy might reach future leaders who, in turn, could improve
the climate for Christian missionaries in their homelands. [1]

THE PASSPORT SKILL

The degree to which we can train New Envoys to cope with
the emerging missions context will determine the degree to
which they can succeed in achieving their mandate.

One basic step in this direction is the requirement that all
Envoys be trained both in the specialized missions skills they
will require (as described above), and also in a separate skill or
professional area that will make them a "valuable commodity"
for the population they wish to reach.

Just as the name implies, this "passport" skill will be the
skill or profession that appears on the Envoy's visa application
and passport. Obviously, the skill must be attractive enough to

motivate the host government to permit the New Envoy to work in their country for a year or more.

Perhaps not quite so obviously, the passport skill must also give the Envoy access to the most likely candidates for evangelization within the target group. Within some countries, one might prefer a skill that would put the Envoy in contact with an agricultural population. In another situation, a scientific discipline or a manufacturing specialization might produce more productive access to a group most likely to be open to the gospel and Christ.

The point is that the passport skill is the admissions ticket to the missions theater. This skill (rather than the "missionary" vocation) will be the identifying label Envoys use in the missions context.

To an increasing degree, the areas of the world closed to missionaries tend also to be closed to many forms of "foreign interference." Thus, the few foreigners who are permitted access to these areas are usually expected to have more than usual credentials.

In a university teaching situation, for example, a Ph.D. would probably be required. In nursing, a registered nurse with a four-year degree and possibly an additional certification might find admissions to the host country and a strategically located placement more likely.

For gaining access to key individuals in the target group, an executive in a multinational corporation or an individual with highly prized scientific or industrial skills might be an excellent candidate to be a New Envoy. In this case, the desirability to the host country of the Envoy's passport skill and the potential level of his or her contact in the host group might outweigh a possible lack of previous missions experience.

Naturally the Envoy candidate would still need the special training described earlier, though much of this could be learned on his own. Such self-instruction would be less than ideal, but the chance to place an Envoy in a key position in the target group might well outweigh the disadvantages.

One fundamental point where Envoy careers will differ from the career criteria for traditional missionaries is that the New Envoys would almost *always* have to be self-supporting in the field. This "tentmaker" (Acts 18:3) requirement would, of course, give the Envoy less time for evangelizing. But it would also produce important benefits.

First, the Envoy's missions activities would be untraceable, since there would be no sending body. Second, the Envoy's passport profession would create natural working opportunities for witness. And third, there would be no need to leave the missions field at regular intervals to secure funds.

The tentmaking requirement is also consistent with one of the basic premises of the New Envoys: They not compete for resources (that is, missions support) which current traditional missionaries require.

Depending on the needs and resources of the Envoy's target group, a wide variety of passport skills might be appropriate. One might teach English as a second language in China or in a Muslim country. A nurse or a doctor might work for an international health care agency and live in Afghanistan, Burkina Faso, or Chad. The host government might seek qualified teachers in such areas as animal husbandry, water conservation, or public health.

A Western diplomat sent to a limited-access country in East Africa might have ample opportunities to hold regular Bible studies in his home.

In a culture where cattle are important (as they are, for example, in India, Thailand, or among Kenya's Maasai), a veterinarian might possess the right keys to open many doors (and hearts).

A skilled relief professional will also be welcome in many situations—and may (as we will see later) experience some of the most fruitful evangelization opportunities of all.

Almost any productive and ethical skill which the target group is seeking and which its members will pay for could be a good passport skill for the New Envoy.

And so, properly selected and cross-disciplinary trained, the New Envoy would appear to be ready for the field . . . but first, one additional piece of training, a new discipline to master (and create): the strategies that will enable the New Envoys to handle the enormous task ahead.

QUESTIONS FOR THOUGHT AND REVIEW

- In brief, what is the "emerging missions context" God's New Envoys must face?
- In your opinion, what are the most essential elements in their training?
- Explain the term "passport skill" and describe a passport skill you already have or might wish to acquire.

Documentation and Notes

1. For a helpful article on this technique see Hal Guffey's "Reach the World without Leaving Campus—Share the 'Good News' With Internationals" in *The Great Commission Handbook 1984* (Evanston, Ill.: Sherman Marketing, Center for Information on Christian Students' Opportunities, 1984), pp. 45-50.

THE BASIC
BATTLE PLAN

IN sending out 100,000 New
Envoys to attempt to reach the roughly 2.7 billion unsaved
people now residing in 77 closed countries, we send them into a
life-or-death battle outnumbered about 27,000 to 1. Equipped
with their Bibles and God's love, they go up against some of the
world's most awesome police states, entering its most inaccessible lands, and facing some of its most devastating perils of
physical torture and disease.

Obviously, they can succeed only with God's help, invok-
ing the same claim Paul made when struggling to gain strength
for his own overwhelming ministry some nineteen centuries
ago:

> But he [the Lord] said to me, "My grace is sufficient for
> you, for my power is made perfect in weakness."
> Therefore I will boast all the more gladly about my
> weaknesses, so that Christ's power may rest on me. That
> is why, for Christ's sake, I delight in weaknesses, in
> insults, in hardships, in persecutions, in difficulties. For
> when I am weak, then I am strong. (2 Corinthians
> 12:9-10)

Clearly, God's grace is sufficient. But we also need to be good stewards of the talents He has given us. To this end, we must maximize the effectiveness of the 100,000 who face such overwhelming odds.

As with any battle, the outcome will be influenced by a number of factors. Two of these—superior personnel and superior training—already have been discussed. A third factor—superior strategy—is the subject of the next three chapters.

STRATEGIC FRAMEWORK

To help develop our overall strategy, we can broadly generalize two kinds of populations in the world today and two corresponding approaches to them. To help us differentiate these

---

THE OPENNESS MODEL

Using four indexes as guides (as shown in the charts on the next page), we can classify a given nation or people group relatively accurately as to its degree of openness to New Envoys.

The purpose of this classification is to identify the openings—and develop strategies—that will best enable Envoys to enter and then evangelize and make conversions within a given country or people group. A quick glance reveals that these indexes represent windows of opportunity—the openings through which the Envoys can enter, even into countries and groups normally considered closed.

Like the tiny "eye of the needle" doorway used as the nighttime entrance through biblical Jerusalem's walls, a single index of three or more may provide sufficient opening for a New Envoy to enter—though certainly not with a passport stamped "Missionary."

The People's Republic of China is an excellent example of the kind of closed country where the government hospitality index is very low, but the people's receptivity index apparently quite high. There is no doubt that, for whatever reason, millions of citizens in today's China appear highly open to a nontraditional missionary approach. We could expect China to be a very fruitful area for the New Envoys' work, and we must study the marvelous growth pattern of Christ groups in China for a possible model to follow in other closed countries.

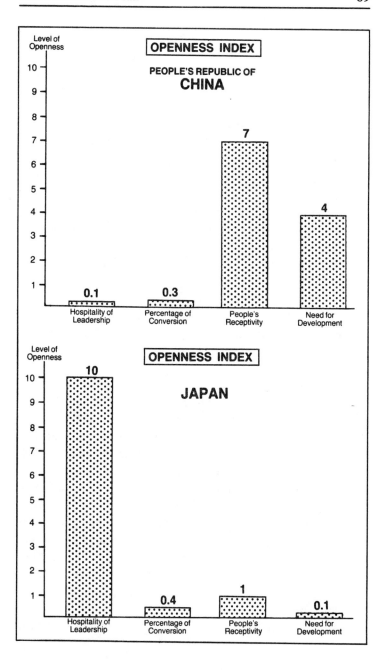

two populations, we'll measure four factors: (1) hospitality of leadership, (2) percentage of conversion, (3) people's receptivity, and (4) need for development.

The *"Hospitality Index"* refers to the degree to which the leaders—of a country, of a cultural group within a country, or of a people group —are hospitable to Christianity. It refers especially to the quantity and severity of social (or governmental) sanctions placed upon gospel witness.

As noted earlier, about 65 percent of the world's total population—about 3.2 billion people (including both Christians and non-Christians)—live in limited-access countries. Many such countries have official policies prohibiting the entrance of evangelists, and limiting or totally forbidding the evangelistic activities of national Christians. These sanctions on Christian witness and activity are placed on the Christian community by the leadership of the larger community of which they are a part.

The *"Conversion Index"* refers to the percentage of people within a given population who would identify themselves as Christians, especially in a safe environment where no persecution would be expected.

The *"Receptivity Index"* gauges how much the members of a particular population or people group are receptive to the gospel. Unlike the hospitality index, which refers to the relative absence of group or governmental sanctions on Christian witness and activity, the receptivity index reflects the relative openness to gospel witness among *individuals* within that group.

In the People's Republic of China, for instance, the hospitality index (measuring the government's feelings) might be a mere one or two; according to recent reports, the government (the social setting) remains antagonistic toward Christian witness. However, the receptivity index (measuring the people's feelings) might read six or seven; the people as a whole appear to be quite open to the gospel message.[1] Thus, hospitality is low, receptivity high.

This level of disparity is not at all uncommon. In fact, it

may be typical of many of the older and more authoritarian Communist regimes.

Finally, *the "Development Index"* seeks to measure the conditions of physical need in a target group and, more importantly, to measure whether there is a genuine need for physical relief and development assistance from outside sources.

Peter McPherson of the United States Agency for International Development tells us that 90 percent of the world's population in the year 2000 will live in yet-to-be-developed countries. This means that potentially more people than ever will be living in an environment where their leadership will perceive a need for relief and development assistance from outside sources.[2]

The establishment of openness scale ratings for a given country or people group will often be difficult and somewhat subjective, especially since in most unreached groups it would be impossible to survey the group's members and their leadership. In such cases, missionaries or New Envoys who have worked with these populations could be surveyed and asked to give their best guesses about the ratings for each of the four scales.

The maximum imaginable level of hospitality, conversion, people's receptivity, and need for development would be scored as a ten, moderate levels would be five, and so on.

Even though the final figures will not have a high level of demonstrable reliability, these "guestimated" ratings will still be quite helpful as a way of guiding us to the most appropriate mission strategies.

For diagnostic purposes, hospitality ratings averaging roughly seven and above should be considered *highly open*. Ratings averaging less than seven and more than five would be considered *moderately open* (or simply *open*). Groups or countries with hospitality ratings of five or less would be considered *closed*—but, of course, still accessible through the strategies New Envoys employ.

As specific countries and groups are evaluated, only a handful would be expected to rate at the lowest levels *in all four categories*. In most cases, even in relatively closed countries, one would expect to see a divergence in these scales. That divergence would create the openings through which New Envoys would enter the country or group to do their missions work.

Over the next few decades, it is hoped that the openness model or some adaptation of it will prove to be a useful predictive and strategizing tool in the missions field. One might imagine a global missions computer somewhere containing regularly updated bar graphs depicting the four index levels for each of the world's 223 sovereign and nonsovereign nations, as well as for each of its 24,000 people groups. Through these models we could predict whether a country should receive New Envoys (hospitality index five or less) or traditional missionaries (hospitality index above five), and whether it should be a provider of missions personnel for other lands (hospitality index of eight to ten).

In addition, the models would help us prescribe the best approaches for gaining access to the country or group, and, once there, for evangelizing with maximum effectiveness.

Finally, the models could be used to measure progress, through updating at regular intervals.

Two Basic Approaches

To clarify our understanding of the wide variety of strategies available to the New Envoys, it may be helpful to first subdivide all the possible strategies into two basic categories—*harvesting approaches* and *preparatory approaches*.

The *harvesting approaches* will primarily be practiced by traditional missionaries—in countries and people groups with higher hospitality ratings (above five). Here missionaries are allowed to enter as missionaries, there is a high receptivity to the gospel, Christians are well represented in the national population, and physical needs are not so great that they overwhelm all other concerns. In such cases, God's Word can and must be shared directly and aggressively.

The world's exploding non-Christian population demands more, not fewer, traditional career missionaries to accelerate the harvesting in these groups and countries where harvesting strategies are feasible. These missionaries both deserve and need the increasingly sophisticated missions strategy training being provided in many quarters. They also need more precise knowledge of the processes by which peoples of the world come to faith and obedience in Jesus Christ.

Because of the rapid urbanization and Asianization of the world's population, many of these future career missionaries will also require specialized training in techniques for reaching specific people groups in the cities and in the more open parts of Asia.

The *preparatory approaches*—doing something now in the hope that people will respond to the gospel later—will often be the approaches of choice for God's New Envoys. These strategies are usually the Envoys' best alternative among populations with hospitality ratings averaging five or less.

Where career missionaries are not permitted to enter, where people are least responsive to the gospel, where few or no known Christians are part of the population, where people are in need of food, basic health care, education, and information on proper nutrition and food production—in these places God's New Envoys can be very effective in a quiet way, by letting their light so shine before men and women that they may see their good works and glorify their Father who is in heaven (Matthew 5:16).

New Envoys, much more than traditional missionaries, will often maintain a distinction between public strategy and the strategies employed in private, on a one-on-one basis with individual prospective converts. Here the Envoy may harvest—but very discreetly—being careful to nurture and protect the inquirer until he or she is strong enough in the faith to withstand the repression that frequently follows conversion.

Often, building a one-on-one friendship works positively toward leading a person to Christ. The multiplication of this process may eventually create not one Christ group, but many. Then, as these Christ groups are formed, some of the same principles may apply that have been found to lead to the growth and replication of individual churches in other areas.

PRINCIPLES FOR CHRIST GROUP GROWTH

For more than two decades now I have been exploring the question of how God brings people of varied cultural backgrounds to faith and obedience in Christ. Naturally, no two cases of church growth are exactly alike. The growth pattern of a church in Punjab, India, differs from that of a church in Tokyo or in Garden Grove, California.

Yet repeated investigations show that several of the same factors are found in most of the case studies of rapidly growing churches. These factors appear to have stimulated the growth of a significant number of churches which have been the subject of my past studies—in Japan, Brazil, Ethiopia, Indonesia, and the United States.

My belief is that New Envoys will be able to make good use of these same principles in the countries and people groups where they will work. In cases where there is already an established church operating within these areas, the same principles could be expected to positively influence the growth of these churches, just as they have in other parts of the world.

In most cases, however, the New Envoys' goal will be to promote the growth of Christ groups. With this in mind, I have modified these principles slightly to better attune them to the situations New Envoys will face.

The following factors would be expected to stimulate the growth of Christ groups:

1. *Growth-oriented philosophy of ministry.* A Christ group likely to grow will possess a clearly delineated philosophy of ministry bent on growth. This philosophy drives every

member of the group to witness to the unsaved and affirms the expansion of God's kingdom through multiplying these Christ groups and, whenever possible, converting a Christ group into an indigenous church.

2. *Dynamic witnessing members.* A Christ group likely to grow is made up of numerous dynamic witnessing members in frequent contact with non-Christians in their community. The leader of the Christ group exerts his or her influence to make sure a proportionately large number of "outreach laymen" are recruited, trained, and sent out into the community. (A non-growing Christ group or church, in contrast, mobilizes its lay leaders primarily for the maintenance of that group or church as an institution—serving on committees, and making sure the group operates smoothly.)

3. *An accurate understanding of itself and its community.* A Christ group likely to grow has an accurate knowledge of its own membership constituency and the community surrounding it. Sophisticated questionnaires and polling techniques are not required here. In most cases, it will be enough for the leadership of the Christ group to know what kind of people have joined the group for the past few years and, thus, among whom it is most effective.

4. *Respecting the lines of communication.* Christ groups, like churches, grow by respecting lines of communication—knowing that the gospel often flows best from one member of a family to another or between two friends. Research among churches shows that the overwhelming majority of most congregations (and we would assume Christ groups as well) have become Christians or joined a particular worshiping body because of the prior involvement of their Christian relatives or friends.

5. *The constant search for God's bridges.* A Christ group likely to grow is in constant search for "God's bridges," and, upon their discovery, develops strategies to reach them. The patriarch of church growth thinking, Dr. Donald McGavran, uses the phrase "bridges of God" to refer to the segments of society that at a given time are most responsive to the gospel. The nature

of these bridges may vary, depending on the culture and the situation, but they always exist. Some examples might be people who have just been divorced, who are experiencing a financial crisis, who have lost a child due to suicide, who are being persecuted, who have become refugees, or who for any reason are strongly dissatisfied with their situation or themselves.

6. *Systems of incorporating and training new members.* A Christ group likely to grow will develop effective systems of incorporating and training new members. Such groups grow when they take in new members on a steady basis, rapidly incorporating them into the core life of the group, nurturing them to become productive and responsive members, and motivating them onward to increasing levels of commitment and involvement.

7. *A high premium on prayer.* A Christ group likely to grow will need to place a high premium on prayer and consequently on the Holy Spirit. It is prayer-led and Spirit-filled. In my studies of church growth in five different countries, I have yet to see a rapidly growing church which has not emphasized intense prayer on the part of its members, both individually and corporately. Especially in the restrictive and hazardous contexts in which New Envoys will operate, a high premium on prayer and the Holy Spirit will be absolutely essential for Christ group growth.

These then are seven basic principles which my research has indicated would be likely to influence growth in Christ groups and, most certainly, in an indigenous church, if such were available.

Now I would like to add three more principles suggested by C. Peter Wagner in his article, "Three Growth Principles for a Soul-winning Church."[3]

While there is some obvious overlap between my own principles and those suggested by Wagner, I think he offers particularly good insights, the benefits of which are well worth the possible duplication.

These three points do not claim to be a fair summarization of his thinking, but rather are abstractions from it, collected to shed additional light on principles that should help stimulate the growth of Christ groups:

8. *A dedicated leader committed to leading his church group into growth.* There is a high price required of the leader of any worshiping body if that body is to grow, Wagner says. The first price: hard work. The second: the willingness to share leadership. This sharing should not take place at the level of top leadership, Wagner explains, but rather at all levels below. Wagner states:

> Gifted lay leadership needs to be discovered and trained
> and put to work.[4]

The final part of the price which the leader of a growing Christ group must pay is "a willingness to have church members whom they cannot personally pastor." This will become increasingly necessary as a Christ group grows or, more likely, subdivides into additional Christ groups. When that happens, the leader

> must be willing to move from what has been called a
> "shepherd" attitude to a "rancher" attitude. A rancher sees
> to it that all the people are properly cared for and
> counseled and consoled, but he himself does not attempt
> to do it personally. He recruits and trains others who are
> gifted for that task so that his own energies can be used for
> more crucial and specialized leadership roles.[5]

9. *A worshiping body willing to pay the price for growth.* The price for growth which the members of the Christ group must be willing to pay takes three forms: (1) "willingness to follow growth leadership" of the Christ group leader; (2) willingness to make generous contributions of their own funds and time so that growth takes place; and (3) willingness "to readjust their fellowship patterns in order to make newcomers feel welcome."[6]

10. *Willingness to seek help*. This final principle is Wagner's suggestion that the leadership of worshiping bodies should be willing to promptly seek outside assistance if that body is not growing. Naturally, New Envoys will probably find such assistance far less readily available than would a pastor in their native land. Yet Envoys who are willing to ask for help may well be able to find a more experienced evangelist who can offer valuable suggestions, and who is already located in the Envoy's area of operation.

I would make two suggestions to the Envoy facing such circumstances. First, the Envoy must be willing to admit a problem exists, and be humble enough to seek guidance. Second, the Envoy needs to be willing to seek assistance, even if the adviser's ecclesiastical orientation happens to be slightly different from his own.

OTHER STRATEGIES

This is probably a good time to make plain that New Envoy strategies should certainly include prompt sharing of all findings about the techniques that appear to be effective in this new and as yet inadequately researched field. In this practice we are following the lead of church growth strategists, one of whose tenets has been that potentially useful church growth research should be shared rapidly—sometimes even at a less-than-fully refined stage—to accelerate the generation of new knowledge.

In the current absence of a newsletter dedicated to the needs of New Envoys, such findings might be submitted to the *Mission Frontiers* or a related publication. Naturally, the bulletin chosen should be instructed to protect the anonymity of New Envoys and their disciples who are attempting to spread the gospel in closed areas.

In such inhospitable circumstances, the Christ groups (including house churches and other quasi-church forms) arising out of the Envoys' work might have to assume more of an underground approach than would otherwise be required. Traditionally, the approach has been that if a person is not sincere enough to risk persecution for Christ's sake, he is not really ready to become a Christian. Under some circumstances, I believe this is still the correct position; but in others, it may not be.

The point is that the mission field of the New Envoys will require flexibility and some compromises as well.

For example, the Christian willing to serve—and who already is working in a closed country—should probably be commissioned immediately as a *pro tem* New Envoy and then encouraged to pursue independent instruction to secure the additional training required.

An agricultural specialist who has already been employed by the government of a limited-access country might serve effectively until additional training could be acquired. He could hold regular Bible studies in his home. Possibly, he could also selectively distribute Scripture and tracts, written in the native ("heart") tongue.

In many situations, New Envoys will need to have the adaptability to work in tandem with Third World missionaries. In 1981, David Barrett calculated that there were 32,500 foreign missionaries sent out by "developing countries outside the Western and Communist worlds."[7]

The following reports by Jeleta Fryman suggest the extent of the expanding work of these Third World missionaries:[8]

- Even after the government of Mozambique turned Communist, one Malawi missionary continued to cross the border regularly, preaching about the Lord. He planted thirty-five churches before the government soldiers arrested him and refused to let him enter Mozambique any more.
- Chinese churches in Singapore sent Bible translators to northern Thailand.
- The Church of Uganda expanded its foreign missionary efforts considerably during the persecutions of Idi Amin's tyrannical regime.

- In spite of intense persecution within its own country, the Church in El Salvador supports missionaries to Spain. And in one economically difficult year, El Salvador's *Iglesia Nazaret* (Nazareth Church) increased its foreign missions budget 41 percent.
- In northeast India, Christians reportedly cross the borders regularly to travel and preach in Burma and as far east as China. While the number of missionaries to India has decreased 40 percent in the past fifteen years, India's own cross-cultural ministry force has swelled to 2,277.
- Significant world missions efforts also are being fielded by the Church in Burma, in Malaysia, in Brazil, and especially in South Korea.

Thus, New Envoys who can learn to work successfully with their brother and sister missionaries from the "uttermost parts" of the world will find their own effectiveness greatly increased.

Missiologist Peter Wagner predicts, quite conservatively I feel, that there could be more than 50,000 of these missionaries originating from the Third World by the year 2000.[9] Hopefully, a significant portion of them will join the effort to reach unreached non-Christians in closed countries—especially in situations where Third World missionaries have cultural commonalities with members of the target groups.

Some new skills will also have to be developed in order to train disciples who can independently create new churches or Christ groups, without additional assistance from the Envoy or an outside group. This is the somewhat elusive ability to produce "spontaneous expansion." The process was described by Roland Allen in *The Spontaneous Expansion of the Church*, a book published in 1927 but still relevant today. As Allen described it:

> The rapid and wide expansion of the Church in the early centuries was due . . . mainly to the spontaneous activity of individuals. . . . As men moved about there were constantly springing up new groups of Christians in different places.
>
> The Church expanded simply by organizing these little groups as they were converted, handing on to them the organization which she had received from her first founders. . . . By a simple act the new group was brought into the unity of the Church, and equipped, as its predecessors had been equipped, not only with all the spiritual power and authority necessary for its own life as an organized unit, but also with all the authority needed to repeat the same process whenever one of its members might convert men in any new village or town.[10]

The actual process of spontaneous expansion is often quite subtle and certainly somewhat mysterious; however, as even this brief quote makes clear, there are always three basic preconditions to the process:

First, the powerful involvement of the Holy Spirit.

Second, the prompt release of authority and control by the conversion agent (the missionary or Envoy).

Third, the willingness to just "let things happen," without trying to control the process or the doctrine, or without trying to take credit for or provide centralized management for the groups once they have sprung up.

Clearly, spontaneous expansion works. It was the primary method of all church growth until about A.D. 950. Also, equally clearly, it requires gospel propagators who will be willing to start the process and then let go, even to the extent of waiving requirements for ordination, establishing "proper" doctrine, and the like.

Here are a number of other approaches that I think will prove effective for the New Envoys:

1. *Relationship evangelism.* Much of the New Envoys' evangelism will have to be expressed in the contexts of individual relationships rather than groups. The style has sometimes been called "friendship" evangelism. It will require great patience on the Envoy's part, building trust slowly and showing Christian virtues more often through deeds than words.

This is what has been called the more "personal" evangelism style of Jesus rather than the "proclamational" style of John the Baptist.[11]

2. *Thinking small.* In countries where the founding of churches is initially both a dangerous and an unrealistic goal, New Envoys will have to think in terms of far more humble worship forms, such as regular meetings in homes or in other relatively safe environments.

For validation of the effectiveness of this strategy, the Envoys might do well to remember Dr. Paul Yonggi Cho, pastor of what may be the world's largest church, Yoido Island Full Gospel Church in Seoul, Korea. It has more than 130,000 members—most of whom participate through more than a thousand Christ groups, led by the church's lay ministers in private homes.[12]

Missionary and development worker John Huffaker, working in the Segalo refugee camp in Somalia, reports that his most successful evangelization occurred while sitting under a riverside tree near the camp. In that picturesque setting, Huffaker held a regular Bible study with five or six refugee men. At first the Bible studies took place inside one of the grass houses in the refugee camp. When things became tense within the camp and the men were afraid of other people finding out about their study of the Word, they suggested the new location beneath the tree.

By being sensitive to locations preferred by the people being ministered to, the New Envoy can not only become more effective, but perhaps also have a more enriching spiritual experience of his own.

3. *Accepting local nationalism and cultural values.* Except where it clearly conflicts with direct teachings of the Bible,

Envoys will have to discard some of their own culturally biased ideas of "proper Christianity" and allow new converts to develop a Christian belief and worship style compatible with *their* culture, and which permits pride in their own nation and its traditions. The goal is to bring the maximum number of people to faith and obedience in Christ.

To this end, the Envoy must give up some personal, culturally biased values so that the resulting Christ groups are truly indigenous, and thus truly relevant to surrounding culture.

4. *Being supportive of the local administration.* As difficult as it may be sometimes, New Envoys must avoid attacking the local government. Their goal is to promote the kingdom and redemption through Christ, not to attack political systems or other religions.

In the long term, only Envoys whom the government feels are relatively harmless to them will be permitted to succeed. These Envoys will need to have a positive message and a positive ministry. Their model should be Jesus telling us to "give to Caesar what is Caesar's, and to God what is God's" (Luke 20:25). Another model could be the apostle Paul, through whom God worked in Ephesus to convert many thousands without Paul's ever once attacking the goddess held sacred by that city's leaders (Acts 19:37).

The diplomatic implication of the last word of the title "God's New Envoys" is quite deliberate. Political savvy is required. In most cases, the Envoys will need to be aware of political realities at the national level of the countries where they work, as well as being astute about politics within the local villages or communities where their ministries actually take place.

5. *Being relevant.* To be understood and believed, the Envoys need to understand the values of the culture where they work. More importantly, they must be able to explain the gospel with analogies that fit the value structure and needs of the people they wish to convert.

As members of the minority wherever they work, Envoys must know a great deal about the dominant religious or political philosophy they are attempting to supplant.

It would appear, for example, that an animist's selection of either Islam or Christianity will depend on the degree to which the "new religion" is made culturally relevant to him. This relevance would not usually be expressed in any philosophical statements from the New Envoys, but more likely by their actions, especially in areas such as relief and development.

For an animist, a development approach which preserved and revered nature and God's natural gifts might be vital. Conversely, a religious approach which attempts to separate man's spiritual development from his utilization of the physical world might have no relevance at all.[13]

Likewise, Envoys must learn to talk the language of need. If they cannot tailor their ministries to the often overwhelming physical and emotional needs of the people they hope to reach, these people will probably not be reached at all.

This point is underlined by the success of an outreach of the First Christian Reformed Church operating within an urban slum in Tegucigalpa, the capital of Honduras.

Early on, the church realized that to evangelize effectively, "discipleship classes had to be related to the needs of the people." Among the target population, 30 percent were unemployed and 45 percent were illiterate.

The church's response to these needs was establishment of the John Calvin Technical Institute. The instructors are all professing Christians with very practical skills. In 1982 when the school opened, 37 students were enrolled. By early 1983 there were 144 students, taking courses in electronics, electricity, tailoring, carpentry, and fashion design. The school's ministry is symbiotic. The classes are practical and geared directly to the target group's need for jobs.

On the spiritual side, however, each class day begins with a ten-minute Bible study. There is a youth program on Saturdays, and a program for adults also has been organized. As of this report, sixteen persons are now attending the church's pre-baptismal classes, and more are expected to make a commitment to Christ soon.[14]

6. *Being ready.* Our Lord must often have been weary in His ministry, yet He was always ready to speak of His Father and the kingdom, whenever the right situation presented itself.

The New Envoy must also be prepared to take advantage of every opportunity the Lord provides to share the gospel. In *The Ethics of Smuggling,* Brother Andrew cites many personal experiences to illustrate this point.

My favorite of his examples occurred when his Volkswagen bus was seized in the Russian-occupied zone between Berlin and West Germany. While searching the bus's contents, one of the guards discovered Brother Andrew's flannelgraph Bible characters and inquired what their purpose was. Andrew proceeded to do a flannelgraph presentation from Ephesians 6 before a room full of Red Army guards. He had time to give a powerful witness before the officer in charge realized Brother Andrew was preaching, and angrily told him to get back in his bus and leave.[15]

In many closed countries, New Envoys will need to have the courage and presence of mind to capitalize on opportunities such as these. God will provide the opportunities, if the Envoy is looking for them and is open to the Holy Spirit's instruction on how to proceed.

Obviously, the missions strategy of the New Envoys requires new approaches, plus great patience, great love, and the sowing of many seeds—with the prayer that God will do the watering.

With this thought in mind, let us look at special New Envoy strategies for people groups where physical needs are great.

QUESTIONS FOR THOUGHT AND REVIEW

• Explain the Openness Model and how it works.
• Name some basic strategies for building Christ groups.
• List some of the strategies for New Envoys which seem most important to you

Documentation and Notes

1. Carl Lawrence, *The Church in China* (Minneapolis: Bethany House Publishers, 1985), pp. 23-161.

2. Peter McPherson, United States Agency for International Development Note: The *1985 World Population Data Sheet* would indicate a lower estimate (79.3 percent) for the portion of the world's people living in less developed countries in the year 2000; but whether the 90 percent or 79.3 percent estimate turns out to be most accurate, the statement made in the text will still be correct.

3. C. Peter Wagner, "Three Growth Principles for a Soul Winning Church," *The Complete Book of Church Growth*, Elmer L. Towns, John N. Vaughan, and David J. Seifert, eds. (Wheaton: Tyndale House, 1981), pp. 279-283.

4. Wagner, p. 280.

5. Wagner, p. 281.

6. Wagner, p. 282.

7. Barrett, *World Christian Encyclopedia*, p. 17.

8. Jeleta Fryman, "From the Uttermost Parts," in *World Christian*, March/April 1985, p. 28.

9. C. Peter Wagner, *The Crest of the Wave* (Wheaton: Tyndale House, 1981), pp. 279-283.

10. Roland Allen, *The Spontaneous Expansion of the Church* (Grand Rapids: Eerdmans, 1984), p. 143.

11. Joseph C. Aldrich, *Life-Style Evangelism* (Portland, Ore.: Multnomah Press, 1981), p. 75.

12. Towns, Vaughan, and Seifert, *The Complete Book of Church Growth*, pp. 61-68.

13. Howard Brant, "Community Development among Muslims," a paper presented at Biola University Symbiotic Ministries Symposium, March 6-7, 1985.

14. Paul J. Bergsma, "Holistic Urban Ministry in Tegucigalpa, Honduras," in *Urban Mission*, January 1984, pp. 40-42.

15. Brother Andrew, *The Ethics of Smuggling* (Wheaton: Tyndale House, 1974).

SPECIAL STRATEGIES TO REACH THE SUFFERING

IN *Beyond Hunger,* Art Beals, former executive director for World Concern, reports seeing a powerful Christian ministry among refugees in the heavily Muslim nation of Somalia.

Traditional Christian missionary activities there were considered impossible; helpers in the refugee camp were Christians, but certainly not missionaries. They were medical professionals, a cook, an engineer, a midwife, a pharmacist.

Yet with extensive training in their skill areas, and with "the love of Jesus burning in their souls—they came to bring hope and health, nurture and nutrition to these refugees who had suffered so much." Even without a church planter or evangelist among the whole group of Christian workers, "the witness was unmistakable, quiet and strong, compassionate and sure. Thousands of Somalians were exposed to the reality of God's love."[1]

A more detailed picture of a similarly effective ministry in Somalia is given by development worker John Huffaker.

After 1.5 million refugees fled from famine and war in

neighboring Ethiopia in the late 1970s, thirty-three volunteer agencies were invited to Somalia to conduct relief and development work among them. Six of these agencies were Christian, including Food for the Hungry.

In a report for the Symbiotic Ministries Symposium at Biola University in March 1985,[2] Huffaker says Food for the Hungry's initial strategy involved setting up supplementary feeding programs in two refugee camps with a combined population of ninety thousand. This effort was directed toward malnourished children and pregnant and nursing mothers. As the relief situation improved, the staff sensed a need for new development projects aimed at building self-sufficiency. Three such projects were developed.

The first provided seeds, tools, and irrigation supplies to groups of twenty families.

The second helped a group of women design ceramic stoves that could cut their fuel consumption up to fifty percent (a vital economy, because of deforestation in the area). Widows without other means of support were taught how to fabricate the stoves and then market them in their communities.

The third project helped establish small businesses—aiding a former baker with a loan so he could build an oven, providing tools to beekeepers to carry on their trade, and assisting refugee widows in poultry production. These small business efforts evolved out of relief projects already in progress.

Much of the design for these programs grew out of consultations with camp and community leaders. The agricultural project, for example, developed from refugee requests for assistance in obtaining seeds and tools. In the ceramic stoves project, appropriate local technology was refined to address the local shortage of fuel. The result was that some women needed to walk only five hours, rather than the usual ten, to secure a typically adequate supply of wood.

In addition, some of the women in the ceramic stove project eventually asked to be taught about the Bible. Somalia prohibits proselytizing and direct evangelization of Muslims, and it was Food for the Hungry's intent to comply with this law. However, as Huffaker states,

> Within the context of our work, if individuals approached
> us with questions about our faith, we felt completely at
> liberty to share with them the gospel of Jesus Christ.

While operating fully within the letter of Somalia law, the Food for the Hungry program in that country nevertheless found ample opportunities for evangelism and discipling.

For example, in Mogadishu, the capital of Somalia where Food for the Hungry was headquartered, the staff participated in an international fellowship called "Christ Church" and also in the National Believers' Fellowship. A Bible study was instituted for several refugees who had secured work and residence in the capital.

At the outset, the government knew Food for the Hungry was a Christian relief and development organization. It was never Food for the Hungry's intention to hide Christian activities from either the government leaders or the refugees themselves. Instead, Huffaker says,

> We conducted Bible studies in our homes and in the
> homes of other national believers and asked or answered
> questions when it was appropriate. At no time were we
> threatened by any of the national population because of
> our beliefs.

In one of the refugee camps where Food for the Hungry worked, a group of approximately forty believers was found. They had been meeting twice a week for prayer and worship—having only one small pocket New Testament for their use. Food for the Hungry began teaching basic biblical concepts to the group members, and provided them with additional Bibles. The group appeared to experience a revival, and some who had left it earlier and converted to Islam were found returning to worship with the Christians.

Through contacts made in the agricultural work and ceramic stove projects, several refugees made new or renewed commitments to Christ. One of these had heard the gospel as a child from a mission school in his homeland. Yet at the time he did not feel he had a sufficient understanding to make a commitment to Christ, and he had prayed for someone to come and present to him clearly the Christian faith. Now in a refugee camp twenty-five years later, "he came to our house to have tea," Huffaker recalls, "and asked us to explain to him what it meant to be a Christian."

Christians in a nearby town asked Food for the Hungry to conduct a weekly Bible study for them. Two believers from the camp traveled to the town with the Food for the Hungry staff, resulting in a small group of five or six who would sit out under a tree or in a grass hut to have tea, study Scripture, and join together in prayer. According to latest reports, this group continues to meet.

Huffaker's study of the process of refugee conversions in Somalia suggests a number of thoughts about strategies that appear to work best in these refugee situations. The following words are taken from Huffaker's report, with italics added by me.

> In working with the refugees we attempted to *live at the same level of lifestyle that the refugees lived*. There were, of course, limitations to the extent to which this could be done. Our intention was to make our home as comfortable for the refugees as possible, in other words, *avoid setting up barriers*. The refugees and villagers were welcome to visit us and did not feel threatened by our lifestyle. In turn, they did not feel uncomfortable in inviting us to their homes. Our grass huts and dirt floors also proved to be more practical for staying cool in the heat of the desert.

> By working initially in a relief setting when the going was tough and by living alongside the refugees, we *established credibility*. People saw the nitty-gritty of our daily lives and recognized that we did not have ulterior motives for doing our work. As we *worked with local leadership and developed relationships*, the refugees began to

acknowledge us as human beings very much like themselves. Our own growth in understanding their language and culture was a continual process.

Our lifestyle within both camps as well as in the capital city created a stark contrast to other relief/development workers. For example, in Camp #2 there was a medical team that averaged four to ten workers. Their lifestyle, their words, and their work were very much in contrast to *the integrity and personal concern we communicated.* The contrast drew some interesting remarks from refugees who wanted to know why all Americans were not alike. It certainly presented opportunities to talk about value differences.

In 1983, Muslim medical teams set up work in many refugee camps. Their clinics were manned by devout Bengali doctors. The refugees began commenting on the difference between these noncaring doctors and our listening and responsive team. Again, *this contrast provided opportunities to discuss religious differences.*

Our ministry seemed to "take root" among refugees or villagers who had previously been exposed to the gospel or the concept of Christianity. Several refugees in Camp #2 remembered the medical work of other missionaries in their homeland. Others had attended some form of church in their past. This background gave them at least a framework with which to develop new ideas and understandings of the Scriptures. On several occasions, we were reaping the seed that had been sown by others in earlier years.

In Somalia, Huffaker says, "we were performing what I call 'tea shop evangelism,'" which amounts

to observing when and where social exchanges take place and recognizing the ideal time for the giving and taking of thoughts, questions, and ideas. It was a matter of acknowledging the human value of those whom we are working with and among, and becoming their friends.

The more we learned from them, the more they were willing to learn from us. There are very few people in the world who do not respond to genuine warmth, interest, curiosity, and desire for friendship.

REASONS FOR SUCCESS

It's not yet completely clear why evangelism integrated with relief and development work is so effective—but it is, as shown by the above illustrations from Somalia.

We can, however, point to several plausible causes for the increased harvest for the Lord that occurs when, under proper circumstances, evangelism is paired with relief and development.

To begin with, there are two very basic reasons a missionary evangelist should feel compelled to be involved in relief and development. First, helping those in physical need is one of the most fundamental duties of all Christians and one of the responsibilities most consistently stressed throughout Scripture. The passages listed below give a good sampling of this emphasis, and I hope you'll take time to look up and think about them.

A Scriptural Sampling

The Christian's Responsibility to Help Meet the Physical Needs of Others

Psalm 41:1
Proverbs 11:25, 14:21, 14:31, 22:9, 29:7, 28:27, and 31:8-9
Isaiah 10:1-2 and 58:6-7
Matthew 5:16, 25:40, 7:12, and 10:8
Mark 12:44
Luke 3:11, 6:38, 9:48, 11:41, and 12:33-34
Acts 20:35
Romans 12:8, 12:13, and 12:20
2 Corinthians 9:7
Galatians 5:6, 6:2, and 6:9-10
I Timothy 6:18-19
Hebrews 13:16
James 2:15-17
I John 3:17

Ted Engstrom, president of World Vision, describes the process of relief and development as "an integral part of our obedience to 'go into all the world.'"[3]

Second, relief and development provide some of the most fruitful opportunities for conversions, especially in countries that would be closed to traditional missionary approaches. It can help us reach large numbers of human beings who otherwise would probably live and die without Christ, by gaining for us short-term access to parts of the world where missionaries could not usually enter.

In *Beyond Hunger* Art Beals says,

> Working with the "new missionary," the relief and
> development professional, I have seen doors once closed
> to the gospel swing wide open. . . . As God's love
> becomes incarnated once again in the flesh and blood of
> his compassionate children, giving the "cup of cold water
> in my name" becomes a powerful instrument for Christian
> witness.[4]

This is especially true in situations involving refugees fleeing large-scale disasters. Wars, famines, floods, and the condition of being uprooted all create a level of dissatisfaction with the status quo that seems to open people's hearts and minds to a rare degree. As they become displaced, their ties to their background seem to loosen; they become willing to consider philosophical alternatives (such as Christianity) which under other circumstances might be perceived as too alien to even think about.

In addition, relief and development allow us to show forth the Body of Christ at its loving and cooperating best. Many disaster relief situations bring together a community of exemplary Christians who, in many cases, are both trained evangelists and representatives of the Body at its finest. The people they are helping experience a superior level of Christian behavior highly consistent with scriptural teaching, creating a persuasive presence for Christ.

Moreover, this presence is heightened by the perception that the government appears to be supporting Christianity, even in countries that normally are antagonistic. This greater public tolerance of Christianity may often be more than temporary. Relief and development allow us to demonstrate loving, nonpolitical, and genuinely benevolent intentions in ways that may persuade local and national governments to be more receptive to Christian missionaries later on. But at least for the time being, the refugees sense their freedom to learn from Christians without government retribution.

Under these circumstances, evangelistic results can be astounding. In 1980 I visited Thailand's Khao-I-Dang refugee camp for Cambodian war refugees just inside the Thai border. There were 130,000 suffering refugees in the camp, of whom only eight families had been Christian at the beginning. But soon conversions began occurring sometimes at the rate of hundreds a day. I witnessed the dynamic worship of the believers there, and had the privilege of preaching both in their church and among smaller groups.

Within months, the Christian population of Khao-I-Dang had grown to 20,000. Why this success?

One reason is the "bridge" created by the refugees' spiritual crisis at losing family, possessions, and way of life. Clearly these people were open to a better answer and a better way. Cynics might ascribe the conversions to the refugees' desires to gain credentials that would make them more attractive candidates for immigration to the United States. Opportunist conversion may have been a factor, of course, but it by no means could account for the massive numbers who came to Christ at Khao-I-Dang and at scores of other refugee camps I have visited.

As I review the studies of conversions in refugee camps throughout the world, a number of factors consistently emerge in those cases when conversion rates have been high:

1. *Quality and dedication of Christian staff.* For staff workers, the refugee camp routine is one of much hard work and

many long hours. To succeed in having a spiritual impact on these refugees who have lost everything, they must exhibit a high level of dedication in their Christian witness.

2. *Ability to get along well with authorities*. Many refugee camps are intensely political, and therefore highly regulated by national or local government officials of the host country. In such situations Christian relief and development workers must develop good skills in working with the officials. Often this involves compromise. It certainly requires a high level of diplomatic professionalism and the ability to coexist with authorities, respecting their right to maintain control in what is a difficult situation for all.

3. *Evangelistic skill*. Since refugees tend to be very open to Christ, the Christian worker in these circumstances must be competent enough in evangelism skills to give a clear picture of Christianity in a manner appropriate to deepfelt refugee needs. An academic approach is unsuitable; refugees are looking for answers, not new intellectual challenge.

4. *Relevance to cultural values*. Finally, Christian relief and development workers must be able to present Christianity in a manner fitting the refugees' native culture. The refugees must be able to sense that this is *their* religion, with a Lord who truly understands their unique needs.

Another advantage of relief and development is the benefit it brings to indigenous churches. If a church already has been established in the area in which we are helping, we can design distribution systems that utilize the church, increasing its ministry and prestige.

In this situation the Christian relief and development agency would function as an *enabler* for the local church. We can help existing Christian churches and missions fulfill their ministry of reaching non-Christians by making available to them needed food commodities, necessary funds, and specialist personnel.

The relief and development agency can function also as an *intermediary* and a *catalyst*. Here we can use our information ministries to "plead the cause of the poor and needy" (Proverbs 31:9 KJV), mobilizing First World Christians to come to their support.

The result is a more vigorous and effective global Body of believers, with greater involvement by individual Christians in a symbiotic ministry that will ultimately bring more of the lost to Christ.

As we try looking into the future, we discover almost limitless opportunities for New Envoys to work in contexts of human need. *Global 2000,* one of the most comprehensive studies to date of the expected status of the world in the year 2000, predicts that as the next century begins the world will be more crowded, more polluted, less stable ecologically, and more vulnerable to all kinds of disturbances than our world today.[5]

More than a half billion human beings are now chronically and consistently hungry, with nearly thirteen million expected to die from hunger and hunger-related causes this year.

Every minute hunger claims another twenty-four lives, eighteen of them children. Thirty-five thousand die from hunger and related causes every day, 365 days a year.[6]

Though some maintain that the world hunger situation is improving, there is no uniformity of agreement on this point. In fact, some sources predict the number of hungry people will double by the year 2000.[7]

I would maintain that the issue of how we respond to the massive needs of our fellow human beings is really far more important than to argue about whether or not it is *humanly* possible for these needs eventually to be extinguished. The fact is that 35,000 people—most of them children—now die of hunger and related causes *every day.* It is also a fact that natural disasters, war, and deadly disease continue at an alarming rate. Nor can anyone deny the potential for cataclysmic suffering resulting from the proliferation of nuclear armaments.

As Christians, we must continue to respond to these needs as best we can, for as long as each of us lives and until the Lord returns. The real question—and our focus here—is how can we respond to these needs while more effectively pursuing the Great Commission?

TACTICS

From my own experience and the experience of others, I will now suggest a number of tactics that can help New Envoys effectively meet physical needs, while increasing the harvest for Christ. The numbering of these ideas is fairly arbitrary. Their actual order of importance will vary, depending on the situation.

Note that the primary focus of these ideas is on development rather than relief. This is because during the relief phase of the relief-development continuum, there are rarely adequate opportunities for evangelization.

This does not mean, however, that the relief phase is unimportant. Quite the contrary. If properly handled, it can create a climate of trust and mutual respect that will make later evangelistic efforts far more fruitful.

The following, then, are ten suggested tactics related to situations of need:

1. *High selectivity in staffing*. In relief and development situations there is always a limited budget, and—in closed countries especially—often a limitation in the number of "expatriate" staff the host nation will allow you to bring in.

This means every expatriate staff member must be the best trained possible, since lives are at stake, both temporal and eternal. Great care should also be taken in selection of the national staff, since they are your best prospects for disciples who can continue the evangelism after the development team leaves.

In one closed country where Food for the Hungry operates, three of our five relief and development teams have been headed by former missionaries—all with fluency in at least one of the local languages, all with graduate level training, and all with at least ten years' prior missions experience in that same country.

The director of our programs there has a master's degree in a relief-related field, has a long-term missions background, and is fluent in the local language.

If this sounds like overqualification, it isn't. These highly experienced professionals (all of whom meet New Envoy standards) cost no more to maintain in the field than novices would. Yet with their more mature skills they have gained the respect of the local officials (normally anti-Christian) and have also maximized the results we can achieve.

2. *Indiscriminate giving*. Hunger knows no religious or political distinctions, nor should development and relief. Aid should be given indiscriminately to *all* who need it. When it is, both the recipients and their government will appreciate your impartiality and will believe more in the disinterestedness of your concern.

In 1982 a combined effort of relief organizations and American and Canadian churches provided a massive relief effort in Poland, supplying food, medicine, clothing, and Bibles. At Warsaw's Polaska Church—one of the main distribution points—aid was provided totally indiscriminately. There was no requirement that the recipients be Christian or even interested in learning more about Christ. By coincidence, the church was next-door to a large police station, so we had ample opportunity to satisfy the government as to the benign and helpful nature of this aid.

The Rev. George Bajenski reports that membership of the Polaska Church subsequently doubled within three years. Bajenski also says there appears to be a general growth in Christian witness in other parts of Poland, and the Polish government seems increasingly receptive to the presence of evangelical Christian groups.[8]

We have learned from Poland—through repeated trips back to that country and from Pastor Bajenski's later interviews—that people long remember good deeds, especially unselfish ones. A genuine act of charity offered indiscriminately to all who need assistance is truly an investment in the future with long-term dividends.

3. *Staying nonpolitical.* It sometimes takes great discipline, but if you want to operate effectively in a closed country, you've got to avoid taking sides. The top priority for New Envoys should be to win converts for the eternal kingdom, not to reform a temporal one. By taking sides against the government, the Envoys risk scaring away potential converts who, after all, might prefer to learn about Christ without landing in jail.

A question sometimes raised is why we help in Communist countries that, presumably, are our enemies. The first answer comes from the Bible:

> If your enemy is hungry, give him food to eat; if he is
> thirsty, give him water to drink. (Proverbs 25:21)

Another answer is that we help people, not their governments. Likewise, it is those same people (not their governments) whom we wish to evangelize.

Finally, there's the perspective of our own national interest. Arthur Simon, founder and director of Bread for the World, makes this point:

> Aside from our moral perspective as Christians, it is not in
> our national interest to use food as a political weapon. We
> do not endear ourselves to other nations in this way. If we
> withhold food from starving people in Ethiopia because
> we don't like their government, do we make Ethiopians
> more likely to tilt toward the West and an open society? Or
> do we make them all the more determined to head in the
> opposite direction? No one can say for certain, and we
> should do right regardless of the consequences. But
> certainly there is a greater possibility that the country will
> eventually lean in our direction if we are perceived as
> people who have compassion for their starving citizens.[9]

4. *Not rushing the evangelism.* Before people from another culture will believe the things we say, they need

concrete demonstrations of our genuine care for them. This is the first reason evangelism should not usually begin the moment New Envoys arrive on the scene of a disaster.

The second reason derives from human physiology. As one medical missionary from Ethiopia put it, hungry people cannot hear a spiritual message "until you get some food in their stomachs."[10]

The missionary's statement, by the way, is quite literally correct. By the time a hunger situation has grown severe enough for the international community to be involved, the realistic possibilities for immediate evangelization tend to be limited. With severe and prolonged hunger, the body literally eats its own muscle and tissue, until all that remains is a skin-draped skeleton with staring eyes and very little capacity for listening or reasoning of any kind.

Such extreme hunger leaves people psychologically devastated. It strips them of the will to live. Loss of hearing, speech impairment, blindness, difficulty in walking, abnormal heart rhythm, and erosion of bone mineral are only a few of the side effects which sustained malnourishment brings.[11]

5. *Supporting indigenous churches and Christ groups.* If the goal is to facilitate maximum conversions within a closed country, we must empower local Christians and keep them in charge. In closed countries, New Envoys won't have much success at bringing others to Christ without a willingness to work within the local organization of believers, in the spirit of sharing and mutual support.

This cooperation with the local church (if one exists) can often magnify tremendously the New Envoy's effectiveness. A good example of this is related by Greg Johnson, a missionary of Christian Missionary Fellowship serving among Kenya's Maasai people.

Attempting to coordinate relief aid during a recent Kenyan drought, Greg approached church elders in the Koyiaki group area inhabited by the Maasai. "I am only one person," Greg said, "I cannot possibly feed all of Maasailand or even the ten thousand inhabitants within this group."

After some time the elders worked with Greg to coordinate a program which would reach ten thousand people within a geographic area of approximately sixty by forty kilometers. Church leaders listed all the inhabitants, distributed the food, and decided on the food for work projects that would be undertaken. One of these involved using people to haul water, mix mud, and plaster the walls of a church building being constructed. In other areas, they helped build an airstrip and constructed cattle dips and roads.

"The church assumed the responsibility, gave of itself untiringly, and worked with the overall committees involved in the appropriate Maasai way," Greg reports. In the process, thousands of people were helped and the prestige and outreach of the indigenous church to the Maasai was greatly strengthened.

New Envoys can place great confidence in national Christians, even in countries where Christian activities are severely restricted. These believers will often engage in exceptionally high levels of personal sacrifice for the sake of God's work.

Brother Andrew in *God's Smuggler* tells about Abraham, a Bulgarian peasant Christian. Abraham earned the nickname "Giant Killer" because "he was always setting out to find his 'Goliath'—some high-ranking party official or army man to whom he could bring his witness. On the many occasions when the Goliath won, Abraham ended up in jail. But on the others, when Abraham won, a new soul was added to Christ's church."

Abraham and his wife lived on wild berries and fruit and a little bread, because their unyielding witness had prompted the officials to strip away almost all their means of support. The lesson from Abraham for New Envoys is simply this: Never underestimate the willingness of the national population to truly martyr themselves for Christ. [12]

6. *Leaving in time*. In development work, we can't stay

on the scene so long that we build unnecessary dependency. Usually when development work begins, objectives are set along with a timetable specifying completion dates. This is another reason it's so essential to train disciples who can continue the evangelization after the New Envoys leave.

Sometimes, of course, the moment of departure isn't a matter of choice, and comes sooner than desired. One veteran missionary (really a New Envoy, without the title) worked to make converts within a remote tribe. When the country went Communist, he was forced out.

Ten years later he was finally able to return, and made inquiries about one of the most promising disciples from the period before the revolution. Almost miraculously, he located the young man, who traveled days on foot to rejoin his mentor. As of this writing, the disciple and the missionary are once again working together, reuniting a partnership for Christ.

When the young man eventually rejoins his tribe, they will most likely have a powerful witness from one of their own, in an area of the world which is unreached by the gospel and almost inaccessible to outsiders.

The missionary's patience as he endured a decade-long wait illustrates an appropriate New Envoy response to a certain fact: In the kinds of populations New Envoys will encounter, severe and usually unpredictable change will be commonplace. Sudden shifts in population, staff illness and failure, and major alterations in the regulations are to be expected as routine. New Envoys must therefore become skilled at compensating for such change.

On September 8, 1981, when the Shikhiu refugee camp in Thailand became a detention center, relief workers who had been working with that population suddenly discovered their presence was barred. Using the seven years' rapport they had previously established with the commander, however, the workers moved cautiously and received unofficial permission to make monthly visits and monthly supply dropoffs.

Similarly, at Thailand's Na Pho refugee camp, long-term workers also found themselves barred. In this case a Thai disciple was chosen to carry on their work, unofficially of course. Because the disciple had been well trained and "fit in" so well, he was actually allowed to conduct a Bible teaching program in the camp during his regular visits.

Battling with the frequent change and almost constant frustration of such ministries "exposes us to the utter darkness, the appalling madness of man in rebellion against God," reports veteran Christian relief and development worker Cliff Westergren. It also underlines "the necessity of the Christian answer which is outside of man and goes to the core of his need."[13]

7. *Visible prayer-centeredness.* Even in a very closed country, the New Envoys, as foreigners, will usually be allowed to pray publicly and practice their personal religious beliefs, at least to a point. So if we wish unbelievers to trust in the efficacy of prayer, we must demonstrate by our actions the level of our faith in prayer and the loving nature of the Lord. Even when we can't tell them what we believe, we can certainly show them. And we must.

In the missions field it will often be essential for New Envoys to conduct their personal prayer life at a higher level of visibility than they might prefer if back at home. Miriam Adeney tells of a missionary serving a Latin American tribe who discovered the Christian converts among the tribe had held a prayer meeting for a sick member, but had not invited him.

Distressed at not being included, the missionary asked why. The answer: "We didn't know whether you really believe God can heal." When faced with sickness or injury, he realized that the villagers had seen him offering pharmaceutical help, rather than prayer.

Adeney continues, "A Muslim prays five times a day, wherever he is. A pagan prays before he plants a field, before he harvests, before he builds a house. When we go to other countries, we must stop our Western compartmentalizing of the

secular and the sacred." Adeney recommends that office personnel in foreign countries learn to stop and pray with colleagues in
the middle of managerial problems, and agriculturists learn to
stand and pray in the middle of fields. In short, New Envoys
need to adopt a religious style which makes sense within the culture in which they are attempting to minister.[14]

8. *No strings attached*. By using conversion as a precondition for aid, we lose credibility as servants of the Lord who
loves all people equally. It will probably also mean getting
thrown out of the country, and deservedly so.

In fact, in a relief situation we must not even think about
evangelism until the real disaster phase is ended. The goal is to
demonstrate God's enduring love, not opportunism. Our best
opportunity for witness during the disaster and its immediate
aftermath will be our actions: serving the suffering selflessly
and turning to God faithfully—and visibly—for the energy and
support we will surely need.

Actions rather than words must always be a beginning principle for the New Envoy who wishes to succeed in the Third
World. Especially in less "developed" areas, Envoys will need
to be willing to invest a lot of themselves in the process.

Miriam Adeney describes the case of Bruce Olson, medical worker with the Motilones of the South American jungles.
At first when Olson tried to introduce simple modern medicines
to these people, they refused to use them. Then one day an
epidemic of pink eye swept through the village. Soon everybody had burning, running eyes.

Olson had a simple antibiotic that would tackle the disease, but the people wouldn't use it. In desperation, he finally
exposed himself to pink eye and went to the native healer, asking her assistance. "Bruce, I wish I could help you," she an-
swered, "but I've tried every herb and chant I know. Nothing
works. I'm worn out."

Olson then pulled a tube of ointment out of his own pocket. "Well, Auntie, I do have some white man's medicine. I

wonder if you would be willing to smear some on my eyes."
She complied. Bruce was cured, and the native healer tried the
same medicine on all the others who were afflicted—with, of
course, the same result.

Because of Olson's willingness to risk his own health and
to empower the native healer, she began to listen to his suggestions. The same spirit of self-sacrifice and a willingness to work
through the native channels will be an essential technique for all
New Envoys.[15]

9. *Cooperation.* It's imperative in relief and development
to demonstrate the highest level of cooperation within the Body
of Christ. Fortunately, this cooperation comes much easier in
the field, especially in a highly closed country where all Christian development workers are more or less on their guard and at
risk.

One case of such cooperation has occurred in the country
of Nepal, where Christian professionals have been at the fore-
front of that country's entrance into the twentieth century. "In a
land that knew no Christians only three decades ago, today there
are thousands of believers in hundreds of worshiping communities all across Nepal—a 'closed country with an open
heart.' "[16]

Art Beals ascribes much of this success to the combined
efforts of Christian professionals (much like New Envoys) from
more than thirty countries, who together constitute the United
Mission to Nepal. Through their efforts, Beals says, "hydroelec-
tric dams, bridges and roads . . . agricultural and community
health programs, plywood mills and furniture factories"—all
have been used to "announce the loving presence of Jesus
Christ."[17]

As a result of these symbiotic ministries, the people's
needs—both physical and spiritual—have been met, and the
harvest for Christ has been both profound and enduring.

10. *Linking up with radio.* It's not always possible—but
where it is, New Envoys can increase their effectiveness by

working in concert with a native-language Christian broadcast
ministry that reaches the Envoys' target population, both in situations of great physical need and elsewhere.

By working together, radio broadcasters and God's New
Envoys can penetrate highly resistive countries and people
groups to more effectively extend the Church of Jesus Christ.
These two types of specialized ministries together hold a key to
reaching the physically and spiritually hungry behind closed
doors. This is one of the most critical arenas in world evangelization today. Creative experiments are in order, so that new and
effective strategies will emerge.

The steps to be taken in such a joint enterprise include
these:

(a) Test the team's compatibility. Naturally, both broadcasters and New Envoys must agree on the basic issue that "man
does not live on bread alone" (Deuteronomy 8:3) and that people
without Christ are lost and in need of salvation. In a similar
vein, broadcasters must regard their ministry incomplete if it
does not speak to the heartfelt needs of the listeners in a culturally appropriate way. Though functionally varied, the members
of the broadcast/New Envoy team must share compatibility of
purpose.

(b) Select a target group. Within the boundaries of the
world's 77-plus closed countries are thousands of people groups
distinguished by cultural, linguistic, and ethnic diversities. Research is primary for selecting several people groups who will
be the most effective targets.

Each people group selected should meet the following
criteria:
- be behind closed doors;
- comprise at least 100,000 people;
- be in genuine need of development assistance;
- and contain a Christward movement in a fairly large
  section of its population (perhaps two percent or three
  percent of the population).

The physical needs of the chosen groups should be such that the development-trained New Envoy can be utilized, and that a ten- to fifteen-year commitment can be made for this collaborative ministry. Here, meeting the physical need does not mean feeding people who are starving to death, but rather developing the ability of the area to grow two to five times as much food. The higher the group's receptivity to the gospel, the better chance it will have to be selected for this experiment.

(c) Focus narrowly on the target group. The broadcast programs must be produced with the target people—their heartfelt needs and their unique sociocultural backgrounds—kept uppermost in mind. The broadcasters must concentrate their efforts narrowly on the identified segments of the target people who appear to be the most receptive.

The programming must reflect the reality of what is happening in the lives of listeners, as discerned by the New Envoys who are responsible for staying in constant touch with them.

This narrow focus on the target group incorporates into programming (among other things) life stories and happenings in the villages, testimonies by recent converts, as well as accounts of the problems faced and conquered by the new believers.

On occasion, the New Envoys may provide transistor radios to groups in strategic locations.

(d) Use the indigenous (heart) language of the target people. The broadcasting language must not be the general language of the province, but rather the specific language of the segment of the population which has been targeted for this effort. People use the "language of the heart" for communicating to their loved ones and friends and expressing their most intimate thoughts—including matters related to faith. Thus, to be effective, the broadcasters must use this heart language as well.

As partners in this effort, both the New Envoys and the broadcasters must be well trained to lead people to Christ, and to help organize them into Christ groups.

11. *Making use of the work of Bible translators.* Substantial progress has been reported this century in making native-language translations of Scripture available to more of the world's people, though a great deal of additional work remains to be done. New Envoys will benefit greatly as these new translations of Scripture become available.

There are an estimated 7,010 distinct and different languages spoken today. In 537 of them, Christian Scriptures had become available by 1900. By 1980, that total rose to 1,811 languages with Scriptures.[18]

As Barrett explains in the *World Christian Encyclopedia,*

This leaves 5,200 languages with no translations as yet—a staggering challenge to global Christianity. Native speakers of these languages in 1980 numbered some 185 million—4.2 percent of the world with no access to the Scriptures in their mother tongue.

Despite the fact that translation projects are continuing at a rapid rate . . . it is calculated that at least 3,297 further languages have a definite need for immediate Bible translation, or at least a probable or possible need; but up to the present no-one has begun the necessary work in them.[19]

In some cases, New Envoys will be seeking to reach precisely those members of the 3,297 language groups still needing native- language Scripture translations. The work of Bible translation ministries will in many cases be vital to the Envoys' ability to reach the unsaved, since the ability to distribute Scripture will be especially effective as a method of outreach in places where the proclamation of the gospel is publicly prohibited.

Well-written tracts in the language of the people will also prove to be very valuable in the New Envoys' ministry. Typical titles for such tracts might include "Basics of the Christian Faith," "How to Organize a Christ Group," "Christ's Way to the Muslim Heart," "Key Verses for Memory," "Victorious Living," and so on.

The tracts must address the issues confronting the people for whom they are written.

12. *A reminder again: Dependence on prayer.* Always worth repeating, though sometimes overlooked, is the vital and indispensable role of prayer in supporting every aspect of the Church's global mission. In the revered King James translation of Luke 10:2 we are told:

> Pray ye therefore the Lord of the harvest, that he would
> send forth labourers into his harvest.

The word *pray* is critical here. In fact, prayer—both by New Envoys in the field and by those who support their global mission—is vital and indispensable at all times. There is no knowing how much closer we might come to fuller obedience to the Great Commission, if more of us would include this vital subject in our prayers more often.

QUESTIONS FOR THOUGHT AND REVIEW

- Describe the special place of ministries related to physical need in the global mission of the Church.
- Explain how as a New Envoy you might prepare yourself to deal with the severe and often unpredictable change which one so often must face in the missions field.
- Explain how broadcast ministries might be used to increase the effectiveness of God's New Envoys.
- Explain the significance of prayer to the New Envoy.

Documentation and Notes

1. Art Beals with Larry Libby, *Beyond Hunger: A Biblical Mandate for Social Responsibility* (Portland, Ore.: Multnomah Press, 1985), p. 189.

2. Excerpts in this section are from John Huffaker, "Symbiosis: A Muslim Case-Study," a paper submitted for the Symbiotic Ministries Symposium, Biola University, March 6, 1985.

3. Ted W. Engstrom, in a letter quoted in *Christianity Today,* October 18, 1985, p. 7.

4. Beals, p. 15.

5. *Global 2000* is by the President's Commission on the Year 2000.

6. For more of these statistics, request a free copy of *The Hunger Primer,* published by Food for the Hungry, P.O. Box E, Scottsdale, Arizona 85252.

7. Tom Sine, ed., *The Church in Response to Human Need,* p. 13.

8. From an interview with the Rev. George Bajenski, November 22, 1985.

9. Arthur Simon, interviewed by Barbara R. Thompson, in *Christianity Today,* September 6, 1985.

10. Jerry Bedsole, Southern Baptist missionary veterinarian to Ethiopia, quoted in *Baptist Beacon,* September 5, 1985, p. 5.

11. James B. Wyngaarden, M.D., and Lloyd H. Smith Jr., M.D., eds., *Textbook of Medicine,* Vol. 2 (Philadelphia: W. B. Saunders, 1982), pp. 1363-1367; and Joan Graf, "Death by Fasting," in *Science 81,* November, 1981, p. 18.

12. Brother Andrew, John and Elizabeth Sherrill, *God's Smuggler* (Carmel, N.Y.: Guideposts Associates, 1967).

13. Cliff Westergren, "Priests on the Street Corners of the World," a paper presented at Biola University Symbiotic Ministries Symposium, March 6-7, 1985.

14. Miriam Adeney, *God's Foreign Policy* (Grand Rapids: Eerdmans, 1984), pp. 25-26.

15. Adeney, pp. 23-24.

16. Beals, p. 75.

17. Beals, p. 75.

18. Barrett, *World Christian Encyclopedia,* p. 13.

19. Barrett, p. 13.

CHAPTER 8

MIXING EVANGELISM WITH RELIEF AND DEVELOPMENT

A missionary to the tiny village of Tubuu in northern Ghana discovered the necessity of a symbiotic ministry in an especially painful way.

Howard Brant of SIM had been a missionary to the village, then was called away. Two years later, he discovered that the Christian converts he had left had been wooed away by Muslim missionaries who also were working in the area.

The greater success of the Muslims was not theological at all, Brant learned, but rather was based on the fact that the Muslims provided development assistance for their converts, whereas Christian converts had received no physical assistance.

"I determined that day that we must find ways of integrating church planting with development," Brant said. "Development is part of the very necessary process in dealing holistically with people like the Mampursi of northern Ghana. They do not make a dichotomy between their souls and their bodies."

Dealing with them simply from the perspective of spiritual need, Brant concluded, did not help them solve the problems they believed were primary.[1]

Clearly, a successful witness for Christ in a setting of human need takes very careful timing and just the right blend of a constantly shifting mixture of these two elements—(1) relief and development and (2) evangelism. The right mixture depends on the situation, and will change as the relief and development process continues.

For some time now, I have been attempting to develop and refine a model that is appropriately adaptable to changing situations, yet heuristic enough to provide guidance to the Christian relief and development worker in the field.

I call this the "Contextual Symbiosis Model." Basically, it suggests that we must always strive for an integration of the evangelism and the relief/development components, and that the proportion of the evangelism must increase as we work our way through the relief and development process.

Within this model, the relief and development process is expressed as having three basic (though often overlapping) steps—all leading to a fourth. I call this the four R's of evangelical relief and development.

The first three R's are . . .

Relief—the emergency, life-or-death stage when victims still are in critical physical need, and emergency medical care is being provided immediately following the disaster.
Recovery—the stage when lives are being restored to the status quo existing before the disaster struck.
Redevelopment—the stage when lives are being reconfigured so a new person can emerge: new in survival skills, new in world outlook, and new in spiritual approach.

Not surprisingly, the fourth R is . . .

Reconciliation—the wonderful moment when a conversion occurs and a new life becomes reconciled to God through Jesus Christ.

In the heady process of attempting to work as Christ's servants in bringing others to Him, we must always, of course, remember that the timing of these miraculous moments is God's, and that God's plans are far more vast and more wonderful than our small attempts to be systematic and structured in our missions strategies.

Having said this, I proceed with trepidation to offer a few suggestions about a workable approach to integrating evangelism into the relief-development continuum. Naturally, it is assumed that New Envoys will check and modify these suggestions—through prayerful openness to the urgings of the Holy Spirit at the time the actual evangelization efforts are made.

At the time of the first R—Relief—evangelism must usually be very subtle. It is primarily expressed as the New Envoys display the values of their own faith—through constant prayer and through the level of selfless, loving servanthood that reflects the boundlessly loving nature of our Lord.

The second R—Recovery—permits better opportunities for spoken evangelism, possibly integrated into lessons on rebuilding and administration of the aid that will help the suffering people get back on their feet again.

Both the Relief and Recovery are stages when the Envoys need to establish their credibility as people who understand and care about those being helped.

For purposes of this discussion, the third step is called here *Redevelopment* rather than simply *development,* the usual term. This is not merely for the continuity of a third word beginning with R (as you might have suspected). The more important reason is to emphasize that even within what some call "undeveloped" nations, the people are, in fact, developed—in terms of their own culture and social systems, which tend to be both sophisticated and complex. "Redevelopment," as opposed to "development," is used here to remind Envoys of the difficult and often painful process of cultural and spiritual reorientation taking place within the new or prospective convert's lifestyle, heart, and head.

In the fourth R—Reconciliation—New Envoys participate in God's divine mystery of conversion. Here it is important for them to remember—especially in foreign cultures—that the little ten-letter word *conversion* expresses an eternally significant process which, especially for the non-Westerner, can result in such an extreme reorientation of values, practices, and beliefs that the new convert may find himself completely uprooted from all that is familiar and all that appears to be secure.

Just because the New Envoy believes in the rightness of conversion does not mean that the process will be any less disorienting—at least at the early stages—for the person being saved.

SYMBIOSIS: A UNIFYING STRATEGY

Over the last few decades, a global battle has been raging between evangelical churches and *conciliar* churches (those belonging to councils such as the National Council of Churches and the World Council of Churches). The subject: Evangelism versus Social Action in the Church's Mission.

This battle—sometimes called "The Great Debate in Mission"[2]—is both wasteful and unnecessary.

The solution for both evangelical and conciliar churches is to commit to *symbiotic* ministry—such as I have described as being practiced by New Envoys in relief and development contexts. This symbiotic ministry blends evangelism (proclamation of the gospel) and social action (meeting people's physical needs *in a nonviolent manner*) into a single, integrated, and vastly more effective effort.[3]

Through the commitment to a symbiotic ministry, churches or members of churches primarily interested in carrying out the Great Commission can work productively and in harmony with churches and church members who wish to minister to both the spiritually and physically hungry of the world. In the process, both groups would benefit.

To make this point more clear, let me define *symbiotic ministry* in more global terms. The term *symbiotic* is the adjective of the compound *symbiosis*, made up of a Greek prefix *sym*, meaning interdependence, and a Greek morpheme *bios*, meaning life. Derived from the field of biology, this word depicts the harmonious living together of two functionally dissimilar organisms in a way beneficial to each other. (This is precisely our goal for both those who favor evangelism and those who favor social action.)

Referring to symbiosis in nature, Linsley Gressit says the term "generally implies a distinct interdependence of two quite different living organisms." Gressit continues, "Symbiosis may be more strictly applied to relationships that are obligatory in some sense: one partner being unable to live without the other."[4]

Thus, following this usage of the term, the symbiotic ministry implies that both evangelism and social action, though separate in function, are inseparable in relations and are *both essential* to the total ministry of Christ's Church.

The only form of social action absolutely excluded from this definition—and which I would personally prefer to exclude entirely from the Church—is social action which sanctions use of political manipulation or violence. For reasons of both effective tactics and sound theology, these coercive methods have no place ever among the strategic approaches used by God's New Envoys.

With this single exception, then, I would hope that churches from different philosophical camps—as well as the New Envoys they send into the field—might be able to find unity of purpose as they support ministries which are symbiotic.

I previously provided numerous reasons why evangelical goals would be better achieved in closed countries by being joined to social (needs-oriented) ministries which take a genuine symbiotic approach.

Let me now outline a few of the benefits to be gained by social-action-emphasizing churches when they also support symbiotic causes and ministries, and when they lend their support to New Envoys who will be utilizing a symbiotic approach:

1. *It's biblical.* As the next chapter will show, the symbiotic approach is more consistent with biblical teachings than one which emphasizes only social action goals.

2. *It works better in "enemy" territories.* Purely social-action-oriented ministries tend to get in trouble with repressive administrations because of the frustration of "not being able to change enough without changing the government first." The symbiotic approach, on the other hand, sets individual conversions as the goal, rather than social "reform." The result is that symbiotic ministries—especially as practiced by God's New Envoys—leave Caesar undisturbed and concentrate on doing God's work.

3. *It avoids parasitism.* Parasitism occurs when "one organism appears to have all the advantages while the other is harmed."[5] Parasitism is often the problem when a more liberal (conciliar) church's ministry gets out of balance—with so much emphasis on the more strident forms of social action that members become dissatisfied and eventually leave the church. In these cases, the first members to leave often tend to be the church's more conservative and more affluent supporters. The solution is support of symbiotic ministries, where the proper balance is intentionally maintained.

4. *It avoids parallelism.* Effective symbiotic ministries, as previously explained, almost never provide a 50-50 balance of evangelism and social action (relief/development). In properly managed symbiotic ministries, the balancing of these components takes place in the field and is adjusted in accordance with the situation and the promptings of the Holy Spirit to achieve optimum missions results. The risk of keeping evangelism and social action separate (that is, nonsymbiotic) is that the balancing often takes place in the church's budgeting process and usually results in a rigid 50-50 mixture which never seems to exactly fit the needs of the field.

Before we go on to review how the New Envoy strategies are consistent with God's plan revealed through Scripture, I close with another illustration of symbiotic ministry at work.

In the hill country of North India, a region containing some fifty thousand villages was known for a high incidence of tuberculosis and other endemic diseases. In 1983 a program was begun to bring primary health care to these villages. Working together with the Evangelical Alliance Mission (TEAM) to develop the three-year pilot project was Dr. Barry Mackey, who was then West Asian director of World Relief.

Dr. Mackey's goals were to reduce the incidence of the endemic diseases, to curb malnutrition, and to provide trained medical workers in several selected villages.

Jerry Ballard, executive director of World Relief, comments on his visit to this area two years later:

> Not only did I find clinics well-established in the six project villages with trained local staff, I found six Christian groups meeting regularly for worship and Bible study.

> It seems that professional excellence, the demonstration of the reality of our Christian faith through action, and our personal witness to the power of the gospel must all find a rightful place in a definition of Christian compassionate ministry, whether we call it relief and recovery, development, or whatever. As Christians we would do well in the midst of much needed social action to remember the words of our Lord, "What shall it profit a man, if he shall gain the whole world, and lose his own soul?"

> Whether it be refugee camps in Southeast Asia, famine relief and development assistance in Africa, working with dislocated peoples in Central America, or wherever God's people have gotten involved—really involved—in the lives of people around them, God has used His people to provide both help for the body and hope for the soul.

> Through our integrated relationship with the churches,
> we've seen closed towns and villages opened to the gospel
> and the church planted on every continent as the direct
> result of faithful stewardship of both our physical and
> spiritual resources.[6]

QUESTIONS FOR THOUGHT AND REVIEW

- Explain the principle of Contextual Symbiosis.
- Explain why symbiosis can be seen as a "unifying strategy."

Documentation and Notes

1. Howard Brant, "Integrating Development with Church Planting," a paper submitted for the Biola University Symbiotic Ministries Symposium, March 6-7, 1985.

2. Donald McGavran, *Eye of the Storm: The Great Debate in Mission* (Waco: Word, 1972).

3. These obviously are abbreviated definitions of two very important concepts. For the full definitions, see my article, "Toward the Symbiotic Ministry: God's Mandate for the Church Today," first printed in *Missiology, An International Review,* Vol. V, No. 3, July 1977.

4. From J. Linsley Gressit, "Symbiosis Runs Wild on the Backs of High-Living Weevils," *Smithsonian,* Vol. 7, No. 11, pp. 136-138.

5. Gressit, p. 136.

6. Letter to the author from Jerry Ballard, executive director, World Relief, January 1985.

THE NEW ENVOY AND SCRIPTURE

To become one of God's New Envoys is to make a major commitment of service to the Lord.

There will be risks. There will be loneliness. There will be much hard work.

Certainly those who are contemplating this vocation should be convinced that the style and the strategies of the New Envoys are consistent with God's plan. As Christians, our best resource for making such a determination is, of course, the Bible.

In this chapter are numerous biblical references for your study. Looking at these references should be combined with a scriptural exploration of your own, plus, something else: the urgings of the Holy Spirit, revealed through prayer.

Earlier we have seen some of the basic scriptural support for the vocation, the style, and the strategies of the New Envoys. We discussed also the Church's biblical mandate for global mission, and saw a list of passages indicating the consistency with which the Bible instructs us to provide for those in need.

Now we will briefly review the biblical basis for some of
the other aspects of the New Envoys' mission and approach.

MODELS FOR SYMBIOTIC MINISTRIES

Beginning with the New Testament, we see in the life of
Jesus a symbiotic ministry in action. Throughout the synoptic
gospels (Matthew, Mark, and Luke), we find Jesus teaching,
preaching, and healing—that is, ministering to both physical
and spiritual needs. Matthew describes the Lord's ministry this
way:

> Jesus went throughout Galilee, *teaching* in their
> synagogues, *preaching* the good news of the kingdom,
> and *healing* every disease and sickness among the people.
> (Matthew 4:23)

Teaching, preaching, and healing were treated as separate
functions, but were all essential components of the total, integrated ministry of Jesus.

The very definition of the Church as "the Body of Christ"
attests to the correctness of a symbiotic ministry—in which
functionally separate elements work in coordination to carry out
God's plan. In his epistles to the Romans and to the Corinthians,
the apostle Paul defines the Church as the Body of Christ, con-
sisting of diverse members, each with its own function, but all
working symbiotically.

> Just as each of us has one body with many members, and
> these members do not all have the same function, so in
> Christ we who are many form one body, and each member
> belongs to all the others. (Romans 12:4-5)

Elsewhere, speaking of the ministry Christ intends for His
Church, Paul says,

> It was he who gave some to be apostles, some to be
> prophets, some to be evangelists, and some to be pastors
> and teachers, to prepare God's people for works of

> service, so that the body of Christ may be built up until we
> all reach unity in the faith and in the knowledge of the Son
> of God and become mature, attaining to the whole
> measure of the fullness of Christ. (Ephesians 4:11-13)

The life of the early Church as reported in the book of Acts was symbiotic ministry in action. In the early stages of the Church's life following Pentecost, Christians were engaged both in proclaiming the good news (evangelism) and in meeting each other's needs (the social ministry).

CONTEXTUAL SYMBIOSIS

In the New Testament, we note not only that the ministries are symbiotic, but that they are symbiotic in accordance with contextual factors.

We see this principle of contextual symbiosis first of all in the life of Jesus, who varied the nature and type of His ministry to fit the situation. For example, in ministering to members of the upper classes such as Sadducees, Pharisees, lawyers, and scribes, His ministry was primarily that of preaching and theological discourses. With these groups He was rarely involved in healing or feeding.

In His ministry to the masses, on the other hand, His approach included not only preaching and teaching but also healing and feeding. And in still other contexts, such as His encounter with a Syrophoenician woman, His ministry was primarily one of healing.

In these cases, the nature of the needs and the audience were the determining factors (just as they will be for God's New Envoys). In sending forth the twelve into a preaching and healing mission (Matthew 10), Jesus instructed them to let their movement be guided by the nature of people's receptivity to them.

Not surprisingly, the early Church's symbiotic ministry was also tailored to fit differing contexts. As long as the Church remained predominantly Jewish, it expressed its faith and life

largely in traditional Jewish ways, such as worshiping in the
temple and practicing circumcision.

When the Church moved into the Gentile world, the new
context called for the different expression of faith and life which
now is known as "Paul's strategy for the Gentiles." [1]

OLD TESTAMENT ORIGINS

As is usual with so many biblical themes, the principles of
symbiosis and contextual symbiosis that are so conspicuous in
the New Testament were actually outgrowths of earlier Jewish
practices that began centuries before. If we take the Old Testament traditions seriously, we note that in the earliest stage of Israel's life as God's people there emerged two distinct forms of
ministry: a judicial-prophetic ministry represented by Moses,
and a priestly ministry represented by Aaron.

These two forms fit our definition for symbiotic ministry.
They were functionally separate, but relationally inseparable,
and both clearly were essential to the ongoing process of Israel's
total life as a covenant community.

The Deuteronomic history fits this pattern as well. It recognized three distinct forms of ministry in the person of Samuel:

Samuel as judge;

Samuel as prophet;

Samuel as priest.

These three offices were functionally separate and yet
formed the perspective of Israel's life. They were also in symbiotic relationship, with each office functioning separately but at
the same time in unison with the others for the enhancement of
Israel's total life as God's covenant community.

Later, the prophetic tradition—especially beginning with
Amos—bore witness to the dynamic vitality of symbiotic ministry in the two-fold concerns of Israel's prophets: on the one
hand, concern for man's vertical, personal relationship with
God (or "the knowledge of God," to borrow Hosea's phrase);
and on the other hand, concern for man's horizontal relation-

ship—"Learn to do good, seek justice, correct oppression, defend the fatherless, plead for the widow," to borrow Isaiah's words (1:17, RSV).

From the perspective of the prophets, we have an intimate, personal, loving relationship vertically with Yahweh, and with Him alone. In the Hoseanic sense of *daat elohim,* this vertical knowledge of God was one facet of Israel's covenant responsibility. Another was to "let justice roll down like waters, and righteousness like an ever-flowing stream" (Amos 5:24, RSV) in one's horizontal relationships.

To the prophets, the two were neither identical nor exclusive. They viewed the two relationships (loving God and loving one's neighbor) as involving two distinctly separate objects, but at the same time as mutually inseparable and as both essential for the total life and full realization of God's kingdom. One without the other was insufficient, and a "vain offering," in the words of Isaiah.

OTHER BIBLICAL MODELS

Commitment—Our model for the total, full-life commitment of the New Envoys is, of course, our Lord Himself. As it is so perfectly expressed in 1 John 3:16-18,

> This is how we know what love is: Jesus Christ laid down his life for us. And we ought to lay down our lives for our brothers. If anyone has material possessions and sees his brother in need but has no pity on him, how can the love of God be in him? . . . Let us not love with words or tongue but with actions and in truth.

Likewise we can be confident of *His* commitment to us. Our Lord's own instructions say:

> Come, follow me . . . and I will make you fishers of men. (Mark 1:17).

> Peace be with you! As the Father has sent me, I am sending you. (John 20:21).

"Tentmaking"—Paul, the archetypal "tentmaker" missionary, proved conclusively that a full-time ministry is in no way diminished by the decision to support oneself with a full-time job.

In the seventeenth century, the Moravians began their longstanding tradition of bringing people to Christ by employing missionaries who were potters, carpenters, bakers, watchmakers, and businessmen.

Two centuries later, William Carey, the "father of modern missions," supported his missionary efforts in India as a shoemaker. "My business is to witness for Christ," he said. "I make shoes just to pay the expenses."[2]

Nonhierarchical structure—Just as in the early Church, the New Envoys will belong to a structure that is without centralized administration. Their unity will come from a common commitment to the Lord and to doing God's will. Their "procedural manual" will be Scripture. Their "organization" will come from their unity of purpose and the dictates of the Holy Spirit.

If all of this seems somewhat loose and disorganized, I would suggest it is no more so than was the early Church—which expanded and flourished with precisely this kind of loose structure for centuries.

Nonjudgmental approach—In advising New Envoys to be culturally nonjudgmental in their approach, I look for authority to Paul's epistles:

> Therefore let us stop passing judgment on one another. Instead, make up your mind not to put any stumbling block or obstacle in your brother's way. (Romans 14:13)

> Be kind and compassionate to one another, forgiving each other, just as in Christ God forgave you. (Ephesians 4:32)

Repeatedly in the Scriptures we are told to love one another (as in Romans 13:8, 1 Peter 1:22, 1 John 3:11, 3:23, 4:7 and 4:11-12, and 2 John 5). This certainly requires that we not judge.

Nonsyncretism—While attempting to bring the unsaved to the Lord, the New Envoy will need to be nonjudgmental about their cultural beliefs which are not inconsistent with explicit biblical teaching. On the other hand, the Envoy must never shun the responsibility to consistently point these people toward God—and away from false religion. There is no room for vacillation here.

Elijah expressed this need to make a clear and firm decision many centuries ago:

> How long will you waver between two opinions? If the
> LORD is God, follow him; but if Baal is God, follow him.
> (1 Kings 18:21)

In conclusion: We have an unchanging mandate and an unchanging Lord. Clearly, the biblical roots go deep indeed for the New Envoys charged to do His work.

QUESTIONS FOR THOUGHT AND REVIEW

- Who and what are the scriptural models for the symbiotic ministries?
- Where is the principle of Contextual Symbiosis revealed in the Old Testament? Where in the New Testament?
- In what other ways does Scripture support the ministry of God's New Envoys?

Documentation and Notes

1. For a more detailed exploration of "Paul's strategy" see Roland Allen, *Missionary Methods: St. Paul's or Ours?*

2. Craig Michalski, "Coming of Age: Tentmaking Is Not Just for Apostles Anymore," in *World Christian,* May/June 1985, p. 36.

CHAPTER 10

HOW TO
GET STARTED

B Y now you have read the requirements for becoming one of God's New Envoys. You've learned about the training they should undergo and the strategies that will help prepare them to work effectively.

You've also looked in on a few of these New Envoys in action—battling fierce obstacles and prevailing in Jesus' Name to bring some of the unreached to the one true Way.

Perhaps you're beginning to feel a quiet, but steady pressure within to get more involved. Maybe the Holy Spirit is speaking to you right now.

If so, it's important to respond. From the stories of others who have become involved in missions work, we learn that the initial inner urgings often seemed very subtle, hard to discern. In fact, for most of us, that message really doesn't become clear until we act.

It is the process of taking action in response to the Holy Spirit's urging that often provides the real clarity. Without responding . . . you'll probably never know.

Remember Paul on the road to Damascus? Surely his vision when the Lord Jesus appeared to him was among the strongest of heavenly proddings. Yet his ministry didn't begin until he received further confirmation through the loss of his eyesight and its subsequent restoration by God through the hands of Ananias (Acts 9:3 19).

Remember also Gideon, whom God instructed to go and save Israel from the mighty army of the Midianites, the first people known to use camels in battle (Judges 6:14). "But, Lord," Gideon asked, "how can I save Israel? My clan is the weakest in Manasseh, and I am the least in my family" (Judges 6:15).

Gideon obeyed God's command, but not until he had been lavishly reassured that the message was legitimate and the Lord's promises real. Before Gideon finally moved into action, God had encouraged him with the miracle of fire emerging from a rock (Judges 6:19-21), and with two additional miracles involving fleece and dew on the ground (Judges 6:36-40).

If your calling to be a New Envoy is genuine, you will surely be confirmed in this calling. But those miracles are likely to come only after you have moved to action.

ESTABLISHING YOUR SPIRITUAL SUPPORT

A first step of response would be to speak to your pastor or minister and ask for encouragement and prayer support. You might also seek a public dedication, possibly in an altar call at your church or in a Bible study group to which you belong. Support through the prayers and concern of your fellow Christians is vital, especially at these early stages, as your commitment to a foreign ministry grows.

This will also be the time to start seeking more educational preparation, as described in chapter 5. In chapter 12 you'll find a suggested list of educational institutions. The course you choose will depend on many factors, including your age, your family status, and whether you live in a country that is open or closed to the gospel.

As you prepare for the New Envoy calling, you might wish to seek the support of traditional missionary organizations. Or perhaps you will turn to a worshiping body such as your church. Although this book has attempted to provide guidance in these matters, you will have to work out these decisions yourself through regular prayer and careful listening to God's unfolding plan for you.

After training, when your calling is both tested and clarified, you may wish to be commissioned through a special service at your church or through a particular missionary organization. Even as a tentmaker missionary who will be financially self-supporting, you should never endeavor to go without the support of friendship, concern, and prayer which a body of fellow Christians can best provide.

Being "sent" to your missions field by the church where you worship has a number of great advantages, even though the sending will most likely involve neither financial nor administrative support.

First, you gain confidence and strength in your calling through a public proclamation of your intent. Second, you receive a commitment for prayer support by those who will be witnessing your commissioning. This will also be the community that you can "report to" from time to time during the course of your service. Finally, by standing in front of a group of fellow Christians and proclaiming your desire to serve as a New Envoy, you will be witnessing to a kind of commitment that may provide encouragement to others.

PLACEMENT IN THE FIELD

One way of becoming a New Envoy is, of course, to already have employment in a closed country or closed people group. Another and more common situation will be to first identify a group or country where your skills will be valued.

Remember that God's New Envoys can earn their living in a wide variety of ways. The apostle Paul was a tentmaker. William Carey made shoes. Other options can be virtually any morally righteous profession that will be of value in your chosen people group and that will be valued enough by its government so you can gain access to the country.

To help you find an appropriate area for service, you'll find a few helpful references in chapter 12. I'm sure you'll also be able to receive guidance and support from many missionary organizations.

One reason for stating publicly in your own church your intent to be a New Envoy is that this will draw out other church members who may have suggestions or contacts that can help you.

If you have never had the experience of bringing others to Christ, you will surely need to seek training in this endeavor. There is a rich body of knowledge available for this purpose which can vastly improve your skills.

Some readers of this book will already have many glorious accomplishments for Christ to their credit. But others have none, and it is my hope that they will be moved to embark on this most wonderful of human experiences for the first time. If you are about to be a first-time evangelist, you no doubt will feel some discomfort, and perhaps misgivings as well.

To be successful at evangelization, it helps to have a good teacher. Such a teacher will hopefully be available through your own church.

In a few denominations, however, evangelistic skills are not so highly prized. If you are in one of those denominations, don't despair. You're in a wonderful position to create a bridge between your denomination and some of the more evangelical churches. I would suggest that you contact the pastor of one of those churches and ask for the training you need. The pastor will be pleased to assist, and you will be helping to bring about a great unity within the Body of Christ.

In the bibliography at the end of this book, I've listed materials you can read to gain more knowledge about evangelism.

The most important step will simply be to begin—to witness to others about Christ. Part of the great surprise in store for you will be the numbers of people who will be overjoyed at what you are offering them.

Remember, however, the sad but true fact which our Lord made clear in the parable of the wedding banquet: Though "many are invited . . . few are chosen" (Matthew 22:14). A similar message is contained in the parable of the sower in Matthew 13:3-9.

You're going to succeed in only a portion of your evangelization efforts—probably in only one encounter out of many.

A CROSS-CULTURAL MINISTRY AT HOME

As the next step, once you've grown more effective at evangelization with an audience that is culturally familiar to you, you will want to develop skills in working with people from other cultures. Fortunately, with the increased mobility of the international student population, this is getting easier to achieve. In the United States there are now at least 400,000 foreign university students, up from 34,000 foreign students thirty years ago. This number is expected to approach one million by the year 1990.[1]

Through this contact with foreign students, you may also find yourself guided to the population where you can best carry out your ministry.

Remember too that most major North American cities have growing numbers of immigrants from Asian, Hispanic, or other nations who are forming clearly identifiable ethnic communities within our urban centers. These too can be ideal target groups for your cross-cultural ministry training.

One special benefit of working with foreign students or immigrants to hone your evangelization skills is that you will be able to take advantage of new techniques that recently have been identified and used with great success to reach ethnic groups in the United States. Here are modified versions of these techniques, which prospective New Envoys might find useful in evangelizing foreign students or immigrants within their own countries:

1. Abandon the notion that the assimilationist approach is the only right way. Current research indicates that the prospect of being assimilated into an Anglo congregation may not be at all appealing or compelling to members of many non-Anglo cultural groups.

2. Focus on the goal of evangelizing, rather than Americanizing or "civilizing."

3. Accept the heterogeneous nature of persons even within each ethnic group. They are differentiated socioeconomically, often linguistically, generationally, and geographically.

4. Utilize the strong ethnic communal ties (friendship and kinship) to the advantage of spreading the gospel.

5. Make use of parachurch organizations for your outreach (for example: home Bible studies and other forms of Christ groups).

6. Attempt to learn and use the indigenous language of your target group.

7. If possible, work in partnership with a member of the group you are trying to reach who is already a Christian.

8. Encourage your church to consider special services or special ministries to support your outreach to the particular target group within which you are attempting to evangelize.

9. Take action—perhaps together with your church—to demonstrate your support of the target group. For example, you might want to make use of one of that group's national holidays to invite some of the group members to get together.

10. Pray that the Holy Spirit will empower you to realize the lostness of every person without Christ and to act decisively to reach some within your ministry group in His name.[2]

OTHER WAYS TO GET STARTED

The corporate witness—If you're currently employed in a secular industry, that too may prove to be an excellent training ground for skills to serve you well as a New Envoy. One advantage of being a "corporate witness" is that you can gain experience witnessing to your professional peers, just as you might be called to do with your co-workers in a closed country. In addition, the corporate environment will teach you how to witness with discretion, since in almost no cases would you be able to use company time and space for anything other than the most discreet and low-key forms of evangelistic sharing.

Employment in Christian ministries—Christian ministries may similarly provide opportunities for training which will be of use to you as a New Envoy. If you choose to work for a Christian relief and development organization, for example, it might be able to provide—on the job—some of the training you will need to be skilled in ministering to both spiritual and physical hunger.

Increasingly, however, these organizations require more advance preparation for their staff positions, less so in the area of relief than in development, where increasingly specialized preparation is desired. This is part of what I hope will be a growing trend of higher professional expectations among the "professional Christians" who work in various capacities in Christian ministries.

If we are going to devote our lives to serving the Lord, I believe we should use every bit of skill, talent, and education available, so that our service can be of the highest quality and make the maximum contribution to furthering God's kingdom. When the cause is good, the quality of staff and their training needs to be excellent, certainly no less than one would expect in a secular job.

Just as you will be expected to be exemplary in both moral and spiritual development as a New Envoy, so also you should attain excellence in your passport skill.

YOUR SPECIAL CALLING

During this "seasoning period," as you practice and refine your skills for the challenges of a closed-country ministry, you will most assuredly be one of God's envoys—doing His work and contributing to the growth and health of His Church.

For purposes of clarity, I reserve the title "God's New Envoys" only for those envoys who are actually at work in closed countries. This is not, however, to denigrate the valuable contribution you will make during your training period, as you endeavor to bring others to Christ.

Hopefully, you will be blessed to conduct your training period amid a supportive Christian community. This will help you move more smoothly through the inevitable maturation process in which you will initially be enthusiastic, then depressed, and finally reach a more realistic understanding of your ministry and what you can expect.

This seasoning period will also provide you with an opportunity to become more attentive to the subtle urgings of the Holy Spirit. As you open up to become more and more trusting in the Lord, you will doubtless find that His leadings are taking you in new directions that may surprise you. Perhaps you will find that your calling is more to be God's envoy to a particular group within your own country, rather than being a New Envoy to an unreached group.

In many post-industrial nations like the United States, Germany, Japan, England, or France, there is an increasing need for specialized ministries to ethnic populations and to disadvantaged groups in urban settings. Within the United States, for example, there is a growing need for envoys trained to minister to the many Native Americans who have left the reservation and moved to cities. If you are a citizen of a European country, on the other hand, you might conduct an important evangelistic outreach to followers of Islam, which is now the second largest religion in Europe.

As always, God's plan is much more subtle and far larger than the human mind can grasp. The very process of beginning your preparation to be one of God's New Envoys will make you a participant in that plan. And if you listen carefully, you will find the Spirit guiding you to greater and greater levels of involvement.

Thus, you must first begin with prayer, then with action, and always with listening, so that you are one with God's purposes. And in the process, the Great Commission will be carried forth.

Early in my career, I undertook an extensive study of church growth in Japan, a study which eventually became a book. The bulk of my research was focused on answering one question: "Just how does the church grow in a predominantly non-Christian culture?"

There were a number of answers to this question, all of which have in one way or another been shared in this book. There was one finding, however, which at first seems so obvious that it is often overlooked. This is, quite simply, that those groups which the Lord blesses with the most conversions are the ones which have the most trained missionaries and nationals devoted to the task.

That's a simple finding, but it points directly at us all. If we seriously intend to spread the gospel of our Lord throughout the world, we need large numbers of people who will be committed to that task. This means none of us can stand idly by and expect the goal to be achieved. We must participate, for by non-participation we could keep salvation from those individuals who were possibly ours alone to reach.

QUESTIONS FOR THOUGHT AND REVIEW

- Would you be willing to serve as one of God's New Envoys?
- If so, what initial steps must you take? And which of these have you already taken?

Documentation and Notes

1. Source: The Institute of International Education and *U.S. News and World Report,* quoted in "Reach the World without Leaving Campus—Share the 'Good News' with Internationals," by Hal Guffey in *The Great Commission Handbook 1984,* p. 45

2. For more information on this subject see Tetsunao Yamamori, "Reaching Ethnic America," *Church Growth: America,* November/December 1978, pp. 4-6, 14-15.

CHAPTER 1 1

THE GREAT ADVENTURE BEGINS

ALL about us a war is going on—the battle for the hearts and souls of humankind.

Whether we like it or not, we are participants in that war. If we remain on the sidelines, we yield victory to the enemy. The forces of hunger, oppression, ignorance, hatred, and death will have gained sway.

God is not forcing us to join this battle. We live in a free creation. But through our Lord Jesus Christ, He is pointing the way. On one side—nonparticipation—is a less abundant life for ourselves and despair for our brothers and sisters whom we might have helped. On the other side is life at its fullest: life eternal beginning now.

A TIME OF DECISION

As I was beginning to write this chapter, I happened to talk with a friend about another mutual friend. Let us call him Philip. Philip is one of those individuals who radiates the heart of Christ wherever he goes. He is the kind of person who, in a closed country, would provoke the question, "What's different about you? What is it you have that we don't?"

As we talked about Philip, my companion mentioned another person in the same profession. He said, "Oh, yes, *he's* the one who brought Philip to Christ."

I was surprised. Then I thought, "What if he hadn't?" Philip's magnificent witness would not be there to show me the heart of Christ which can be in us all. My friend Philip is a saved and manifestly special human being, because one of God's fishermen brought him into the net.

Then I remembered the *other* Philip who was also brought in, as were Matthew, John, Peter, Thaddaeus, and the others. In every case it took a human being acting as an "envoy" of the Father to pass on that spark of salvation—which could then be passed by them to others, who passed it on as well.

We each hold within our heads and hearts the ability to expand the kingdom to the parts of the world we touch. We can each magnify the purpose of our own lives by passing along that divine understanding of Truth to others.

The company of God's New Envoys is just one of the units in Christ's mighty army where we might spend our lives, increasing the riches of humankind. However, it is a very special unit which requires an immediate enlistment of 100,000 trained and able workers for our Lord.

Christ's army is the only army in the world in which the soldiers bring life—not death. It is the only army in which those conquered are set free.

Likewise, it is the only army strong enough to strip the unspeakable violence from those who use terrorism and death to achieve their ends.

Within us all, I am convinced, there is a deep need to make a contribution to good. There is a need to bring hope where there is darkness now—to bring life where all around we see the encroachment of death. This need can be met as one of God's New Envoys.

THE PRICELESS REWARDS

As a New Envoy in a closed country, one can achieve unmatched, unequaled experiences of the power of Christ. Even in more open lands, you will see the miracles of redemption and rebirth unfold again and again before your eyes.

Some of this majesty of Christ's Church in a closed land is revealed through Carl Lawrence's stories collected from persecuted Christians in China. Others exist in the witness of Brother Andrew and in the inspiring stories of Christian political prisoners whose lights burn brightly in the frozen desolation of the Gulag Archipelago.

If you accept this challenge and follow through with your training, and then are placed as a New Envoy in a closed land, you will discover for yourself precisely what Lawrence, Brother Andrew, and the others are talking about.

I can think of no thrill to equal the magnificence of Christian witness in countries where witness means persecution, and sometimes death.

The Church which is battling the darkness is the Church which reveals God's will in a very special way. Oh, if I could only share with you the joy I myself have experienced kneeling in prayer with rain-drenched refugees along the Cambodian border. Or walking into one of our outposts in East Africa and hearing new converts singing "Amazing Grace."

I remember the eyes of so many physically impoverished folk I have seen, as they begin to learn about the Lord. Let me tell you, only as we are able to share the gift of the gospel with the poor and needy do we understand, through their eyes and their excitement, the truly blessed gift Christ has given us all.

As a child in Japan, I used to read the stories of the *ronin,* the masterless warriors who engaged in deeds of bravery with their flashing *katana,* the magnificent long and deadly Japanese swords. In many other parts of the world that same excitement is shared in the stories of the North American cowboy, battling with blazing six-guns and smashing fists.

Those stories were thrilling, but there was something missing. What was missing became clear as we learned about other heroes. In Japan, the real heroes were the *samurai*. They were warriors, too, but they had a purpose in life and a master to serve.

In America, the greater heroes were the U.S. marshals. They were as fast and as tough as the cowboy, but they served peace, justice, and law.

Whether we like it or not, in this creation we are all in the service of some master. Sometimes the master is wealth, sometimes greed, sometimes chaos and evil.

As Christians we have the power to choose the one Master who provides true freedom and eternal, abundant life. Our Lord Jesus Christ is also the only Master who will be with us always—in our joy and in our deepest travail.

As Christians we have already accepted that Master in one sense. But there is another level of acceptance which comes as we move forward in His army and dedicate our lives and activities to service for Him. This is when the greatest miracles begin. This is when Christ's presence before us and within us intensifies and multiplies, and becomes a constant part of our being.

Dream with me of the day when "The Lord shall be King over all the earth," of that day when "His feet will stand on the Mount of Olives," and "living waters shall flow from Jerusalem" (Zechariah 14:9, 14:4, and 14:8, NKJV).

Then, if you will, please stand with the disciples, the apostles, and all those thousands of brave missionaries who have gone before and are working now to spread the kingdom of God to "every tribe and language and people and nation" (Revelation 5:9).

If you take action now, you can reach some of those who may be able to respond only to the special gifts our Lord has given you alone. And through those you reach, others will be saved. And through them, many more.

As of this writing, there are 3.3 billion human beings throughout the world who have not yet been led to the only true Way. Of these, about 2.7 billion are in the 77 restricted access countries where they cannot be reached without a very special effort, such as can be undertaken only by God's New Envoys.

Let us remember always the world white for harvest. The great adventure now before us is to be laborers in God's fields.

I pray, and I ask you to join me, that the Lord of the harvest will send out laborers into His harvest, and that perhaps one of those laborers will be you. And I pray that through your participation, "This gospel of the kingdom shall be preached in the whole world for a witness to all the nations, and then the end shall come" (Matthew 24:14 NASB).

Amen.

QUESTIONS FOR THOUGHT AND REVIEW

- Explore some of the urgings of the Holy Spirit you have experienced in your own life related to the missions field. You might wish to write these down on a sheet of paper in order to explore them further. Feel free to keep them to yourself if you wish.
- Describe how you have responded to these urgings and whether you feel a further response would be appropriate.
- Imagine how you might feel if you were a New Envoy in a country like China or Ethiopia right now. Explore some of these feelings in your mind, and try to imagine what your typical day and typical week would be like.
- Take a moment to pray to ask God's guidance about how you should proceed with the new insights you have gained about yourself and God's plan for you through reading this book.

FOR MORE HELP: RESOURCES FOR NEW ENVOYS

ONE conspicuous omission in resources for God's New Envoys is a central clearing house which will both provide them with information and maintain records about them and their work. It is hoped that one person who reads this book will be moved to establish just such a resource.

Until then, may the information in this chapter serve as a guide to resources for you.

SUGGESTED SCHOOLS

Once you make the decision to become a New Envoy, the best solution for your training needs will depend on your situation. If time and funds are available, it would be desirable for all Envoys to be trained within a formal academic setting.

The following lists of suggested institutions include both schools and training programs available in the United States. They have been prepared primarily by the Lake Wales Consultation Task Force: Doug Millham, World Vision, committee chairperson.

The *"Christian Schools for Cross-Cultural Training"* were either recommended by highly respected sources or were believed noteworthy because of the large number of mission courses they offered.

The list of *"Christian Schools for Relief and Development Training"* reflects only those schools which the Task Force had been able to identify as of press time.

The *"Secular Schools for Relief and Development Training"* were recommended by respected professors teaching in that area of study. This listing is by no means complete; it had to be shortened due to the large number of such programs available.

The *"Secular Schools for Training in International Health"* were recommended by specialists in the field and through the literature on missionary medicine.

These lists of suggested schools and training programs are *by no means exhaustive,* and, with one exception, are restricted to institutions in the United States. For prospective New Envoys residing in other countries, it is hoped that some of these listed institutions can help provide information about resources closer to home.

For more detailed information about educational resources for God's New Envoys, readers are encouraged to consult Doug Millham's published report on the findings of the Lake Wales Task Force, entitled *Lake Wales Consultation Manual* (Monrovia, Calif.: MARC, 1986).

CHRISTIAN SCHOOLS FOR CROSS-CULTURAL TRAINING

Asbury Theological Seminary
North Lexington
Wilmore, KY 40390
606-858-3581

Biola University
13800 Biola Avenue
La Mirada, CA 90639
213-944-0351

Columbia Bible College
P.O. Box 3122
Columbia, SC 29230
803-754-4100

Dallas Theological Seminary
3909 Swiss Avenue
Dallas, TX 75204
214-824-3094

Fuller Theological Seminary
135 N. Oakland Ave.
Pasadena, CA 91101-1790
818-449-1745

Gordon-Conwell Theological Seminary
South Hamilton, MA 01982
617-468-7111

Missionary Internship
P.O. Box 457
Farmington, MI 48024
313-474-9110

Multnomah School of the Bible
8435 N.E. Glisan St.
Portland, OR 97220-5898
503-255-0332

Nazarene Theological Seminary
1700 E. Meyer Boulevard
Kansas City, MO 64131
816-333-6254

Prairie Bible Institute
Three Hills, Alberta
Canada T0M 2A0
403-443-5511

Southwestern Baptist Theological Seminary
P.O. Box 22206
Fort Worth, TX 76122
817-923-1921 Ext. 750

Trinity Evangelical Divinity School
2065 Half Day Road
Deerfield, IL 60015
312-945-8800

Western Conservative Baptist Seminary
5511 S.E. Hawthorne Blvd.
Portland, OR 97215
503-233-8561

Wheaton College
HNGR Program
Wheaton, IL 60187
312-260-5199

OTHER RESOURCES FOR CROSS-CULTURAL TRAINING

East-West Center
Institute of Culture & Communication
1777 East-West Road
Honolulu, HI 96848
808-944-7666

SIETAR (Society for Intercultural Education
   Training and Research)
1414 22nd Street N.W. Suite 102
Washington, DC 20037
202-296-4710

Stanford Institute for Intercultural Communication
P.O. Box A-D
Stanford, CA 94305
415-497-1897

CHRISTIAN SCHOOLS FOR RELIEF AND DEVELOPMENT TRAINING

Goshen College
Division of International Education
Goshen, IN 46526
219-533-3161

Warner Southern College & Food for the Hungry
HEART Program
Lake Wales, FL 33853
813-638-1188 or 1426

Loma Linda University
Riverside, CA 92515
714-785-2176

Oral Roberts University
7777 South Lewis Avenue
Tulsa, OK 74171
918-495-6807

Wheaton College
HNGR Program
Wheaton, IL 60187
312-260-5199

William Carey International University
1539 East Howard Street
Pasadena, CA 91104
818-797-1200

SECULAR SCHOOLS FOR RELIEF AND DEVELOPMENT TRAINING

University of Arizona
Tucson, AZ 85721
602-621-2211

Auburn University
Auburn, AL 36830
205-826-4000

University of California Los Angeles
African Studies Center
Development Institute
10244 Bunche Hall
Los Angeles, CA 90024
213-825-3686

California State University Consortium
3801 W. Temple Avenue
Pomona, CA 91768

University of California Riverside
990 University Avenue
Riverside, CA 92521
714-787-1012

Cornell University
International Agriculture
N.Y.S. College of Agriculture & Life Science
122 Roberts Hall
Ithaca, NY 14853
607-255-1000

University of Florida
1001 McCarthy Hall
Gainesville, FL 32611
904-392-3261

Virginia Polytechnical Institute
Department of International Programs
Blacksburg, VA 24061

SECULAR SCHOOLS FOR TRAINING IN INTERNATIONAL HEALTH

University of California Los Angeles
Dr. Alfred Newman
School of Public Health, Medicine & Nursing
405 Hilgard Avenue
Los Angeles, CA 90024
213-825-5516

University of Hawaii of Manoa
183 Kalakaua Avenue, Suite 700
Honolulu, HI 96815
808-948-8643

John Hopkins School of Public Health
615 N. Wolfe Street
Baltimore, MD 21205
301-955-5000

Michigan State University
East Lansing, MI 48824
517-355-1855

Tulane University
6823 St. Charles Avenue
New Orleans, LA 70118
504-588-5199

OTHER CONTACTS FOR ASSISTANCE

It is of prime importance that God's New Envoys be able to support one another. Though global geography will often make a physical meeting impossible, it is still essential that mutual support among Envoys be accomplished in two important ways:

First, through prayer.

Second, by sharing research promptly.

New Envoys who are already in the field may wish to consider writing and publishing some of their experiences working in this challenging new area.

Some of the publications which might be interested in these submissions include the following:

Christianity Today
465 Gundersen Drive
Carol Stream, IL 60188

Eternity
1716 Spruce Street
Philadelphia, PA 19103

Evangelical Missions Quarterly
Evangelical Missions Information Service, Inc.
25 W. 560 Geneva Road
Box 794
Wheaton, IL 60187

Global Church Growth Bulletin
25 Corning Avenue
Milpitas, CA 95035

International Bulletin of Missionary Research
6315 Ocean Avenue
Ventnor, NJ 08406

Missiology
616 Walnut Avenue
Scottdale, PA 15683-1999

Mission Frontiers
Bulletin of the U.S. Center for World Mission
1605 Elizabeth Street
Pasadena, CA 91104

World Christian
P. O. Box 5199
Chatsworth, CA 91313

Or, possibly, a publication of your own church or denomination.

If you choose to submit a manuscript to one of these publications, it is always good practice to retain a copy of that manuscript for yourself. In addition, it is recommended that you include a self-addressed, stamped envelope so the editors can get back in touch with you.

Naturally, you should always attach name and address, being careful to specify if your name is to be withheld to protect your anonymity in the field.

Articles need not be long. In fact, your chances of publication may be better if the material you send is concisely written and overall quite short.

ADDITIONAL HELPS

If you wish additional information about God's New Envoys or how you might be more effective as a member of their ranks, please feel free to write to me at either of these addresses:

Food for the Hungry, Inc.
P.O. Box E
Scottsdale, AZ 85252-9987
U.S.A.

or

Food for the Hungry International
108 route de Suisse
1290 Versoix/Geneva
Switzerland

If you're looking for an appropriate mission field and have no other contacts, here are a few resources which can get you started in the right direction.

To help mission-motivated Christians in finding salaried, secular employment or study options abroad, contact:

Ruth Siemens
Global Opportunities
1594 North Allen, # 7
Pasadena, CA 91104

or

Tentmakers International
19303 Fremont Avenue
North Seattle, WA 98133

Once you have a certain country or region or people group in mind as a target for your personal ministry, find out as much as possible about the indigenous churches within that target group. This kind of information can be sought from many of the various sources listed above. Remember that even many highly restricted countries have believers in significant numbers. Where there is a Christian presence, never pretend it doesn't exist.

Further information to help you secure employment in a strategic position overseas might come from professional organizations in your vocational area, especially Christian professional organizations. For example, if you are a medical or premedical student or a practicing physician or other health-care worker, you may wish to contact the Christian Medical Society; law students and lawyers could contact the Christian Legal Society, and so on. It would be wise to obtain as much information as possible about overseas work from any professional organization in your field with which you can make contact.

Some of your contacts in your target country, both for professional purposes and for linking up with believers, can come through relationships established with foreign students or immigrants from that country with whom you develop relationships in the United States.

For additional information on the "Hamilton Tentmaker Survey" mentioned at the conclusion of chapter 4, contact:

Mr. Don Hamilton, Director
TMQ Research
312 Melcanyon Road
Duarte, CA 91010

In addition to the academic institutions listed on the preceding pages, a helpful, all-purpose contact for assistance would be the

U.S. Center for World Mission
1605 Elizabeth Street
Pasadena, CA 91104

And finally, all those considering overseas missions work are strongly encouraged to attend the Urbana Convention, the largest student missions convention in North America, held every four years in Urbana, Illinois, and organized through another helpful contact:

Inter-Varsity Christian Fellowship
233 Langdon Street
Madison, WI 53703

A P P E N D I X

A HELPFUL PHILOSOPHY: THE LAUSANNE COVENANT

IN this book I have attempted to provide a basic philosophy for God's New Envoys. I have taken pains that this philosophy be non-restrictive enough to be incorporated into the belief systems of prospective Envoys from a wide range of Christian backgrounds.

For some, this freedom from elaborate philosophy boundaries will be seen as a blessing. It will permit them, through prayer and scriptural study, to build a philosophical infrastructure that best fits the purposes that the Holy Spirit has ordained for them. For others, there may be a desire for a more elaborate positioning statement which they can respond to in developing a philosophy of their own.

For the benefit of this latter group I have received permission to reprint the philosophical position paper which I personally find quite helpful in orienting my own thinking about the mission of the Church: the now famous Lausanne Covenant, one of the products of the International Congress on World Evangelization at Lausanne, Switzerland, in July 1974.

There were 2,700 participants from more than 150 nations at the Congress, and more than half of those present came from the Third World. The meeting was reported by *Time* magazine as "a formidable forum, possibly the widest-ranging meeting of Christians ever held."

I hope you will find this Covenant helpful as an instrument for refining your own missions thinking. Of particular value is its international and culturally nonjudgmental perspective which, to me, is essential to any who would serve as one of God's New Envoys.

THE LAUSANNE COVENANT

Adopted 1974 by the International Congress on World Evangelization, Lausanne, Switzerland.

INTRODUCTION

We, members of the Church of Jesus Christ, from more than 150 nations, participants in the International Congress on World Evangelization at Lausanne, praise God for his great salvation and rejoice in the fellowship he has given us with himself and with each other.

We are deeply stirred by what God is doing in our day, moved to penitence by our failures and challenged by the unfinished task of evangelization.

We believe the Gospel is God's good news for the whole world, and we are determined by his grace to obey Christ's commission to proclaim it to all mankind and to make disciples of every nation. We desire, therefore, to affirm our faith and our resolve, and to make public our covenant.

1. THE PURPOSE OF GOD

We affirm our belief in the one eternal God, Creator and Lord of the world, Father, Son and Holy Spirit, who governs all things according to the purpose of his will. He has been calling out from the world a people for himself, and sending his people back into the world to be his servants and his witnesses, for the extension of his kingdom, the building up of Christ's body, and the glory of his name.

We confess with shame that we have often denied our calling and failed in our mission, by becoming conformed to the world or by withdrawing from it. Yet we rejoice that even when borne by earthen vessels the Gospel is still a precious treasure. To the task of making that treasure known in the power of the Holy Spirit we desire to dedicate ourselves anew.

2. THE AUTHORITY AND POWER OF THE BIBLE

We affirm the divine inspiration, truthfulness and authority of both Old and New Testament Scriptures in their entirety as the only written Word of God, without error in all that it affirms, and the only infallible rule of faith and practice. We also affirm the power of God's Word to accomplish his purpose of salvation.

The message of the Bible is addressed to all mankind, for God's revelation in Christ and in Scripture is unchangeable. Through it the Holy Spirit still speaks today. He illumines the minds of God's people in every culture to perceive its truth freshly through their own eyes, and thus discloses to the whole church ever more of the many-colored wisdom of God.

3. THE UNIQUENESS AND UNIVERSALITY OF CHRIST

We affirm that there is only one Savior and only one Gospel, although there is a wide diversity of evangelistic approaches.

We recognize that all men have some knowledge of God through his general revelation in nature. But we deny that this can save, for men suppress the truth by their unrighteousness. We also reject as derogatory to Christ and the Gospel every kind of syncretism and dialogue which implies that Christ speaks equally through all religions and ideologies. Jesus Christ, being himself the only God-man, who gave himself as the only ransom for sinners, is the only mediator between God and man. There is no other name by which we must be saved.

All men are perishing because of sin, but God loves all men, not wishing that any should perish but that all should repent. Yet those who reject Christ repudiate the joy of salvation and condemn themselves to eternal separation from God. To proclaim Jesus as "the Savior of the world" is not to affirm that all men are either automatically or ultimately saved, still less to affirm that all religions offer salvation in Christ. Rather it is to proclaim God's love for a world of sinners and to invite all men to respond to him as Savior and Lord in the wholehearted personal commitment of repentance and faith.

Jesus Christ has been exalted above every other name; we long for the day when every knee shall bow to him and every tongue shall confess him Lord.

4. The Nature of Evangelism

To evangelize is to spread the good news that Jesus Christ died for our sins and was raised from the dead according to the Scriptures, and that as the reigning Lord he now offers the forgiveness of sins and the liberating gift of the Spirit to all who repent and believe.

Our Christian presence in the world is indispensable to evangelism, and so is that kind of dialogue whose purpose is to listen sensitively in order to understand. But evangelism itself is the proclamation of the historical, biblical Christ as Savior and Lord, with a view to persuading people to come to him personally and so be reconciled to God.

In issuing the Gospel invitation we have no liberty to conceal the cost of discipleship. Jesus still calls all who would follow him to deny themselves, take up their cross, and identify themselves with his new community. The results of evangelism include obedience to Christ, incorporation into his church and responsible service in the world.

5. CHRISTIAN SOCIAL RESPONSIBILITY

We affirm that God is both the Creator and the Judge of all men. We therefore should share his concern for justice and reconciliation throughout human society and for the liberation of men from every kind of oppression.

Because mankind is made in the image of God, every person, regardless of race, religion, color, culture, class, sex, or age, has an intrinsic dignity because of which he should be respected and served, not exploited. Here too we express penitence both for our neglect and for having sometimes regarded evangelism and social concern as mutually exclusive. Although reconciliation with man is not reconciliation with God, nor is social action evangelism, nor is political liberation salvation, nevertheless we affirm that evangelism and socio-political involvement are both part of our Christian duty. For both are necessary expressions of our doctrines of God and man, our love for our neighbor and our obedience to Jesus Christ.

The message of salvation implies also a message of judgment upon every form of alienation, oppression and discrimination, and we should not be afraid to denounce evil and injustice wherever they exist. When people receive Christ they are born again into his kingdom and must seek not only to exhibit but also to spread its righteousness in the midst of an unrighteous world. The salvation we claim should be transforming us in the totality of our personal and social responsibilities. Faith without works is dead.

6. THE CHURCH AND EVANGELISM

We affirm that Christ sends his redeemed people into the world as the Father sent him, and that this calls for a similar deep and costly penetration of the world. We need to break out of our ecclesiastical ghettos and permeate non-Christian society.

In our church's mission of sacrificial service, evangelism is primary. World evangelization requires the whole church to take the whole Gospel to the whole world. The church is at the very center of God's cosmic purpose and is his appointed means of spreading the Gospel. But a church which preaches the Cross must itself be marked by the Cross. It becomes a stumbling block to evangelism when it betrays the Gospel or lacks a living faith in God, a genuine love for people, or scrupulous honesty in all things including promotion and finance.

The church is the community of God's people rather than an institution, and must not be identified with any particular culture, social or political system, or human ideology.

7. COOPERATION IN EVANGELISM

We affirm that the church's visible unity in truth is God's purpose. Evangelism also summons us to unity, because our oneness strengthens our witness, just as our disunity undermines our Gospel of reconciliation. We recognize, however, that organizational unity may take many forms and does not necessarily forward evangelism. Yet we who share the same biblical faith should be closely united in fellowship, work and witness.

We confess that our testimony has sometimes been marred by sinful individualism and needless duplication. We pledge ourselves to seek a deeper unity in truth, worship, holiness and mission. We urge the development of regional and functional cooperation for the furtherance of the church's mission, for strategic planning, for mutual encouragement, and for the sharing of resources and experience.

8. CHURCHES IN EVANGELISTIC PARTNERSHIP

We rejoice that a new missionary era has dawned. The dominant role of western missions is fast disappearing. God is raising up from the younger churches a great new resource for world evangelization, and is thus demonstrating that the responsibility to evangelize belongs to the whole body of Christ. All churches should therefore be asking God and themselves what they should be doing both to reach their own area and to send missionaries to other parts of the world. A reevaluation of our missionary responsibility and role should be continuous. Thus a growing partnership of churches will develop and the universal character of Christ's church will be more clearly exhibited.

We also thank God for agencies which labor in Bible translation, theological education, the mass media, Christian literature, evangelism, missions, church renewal and other specialist fields. They too should engage in constant self-examination to evaluate their effectiveness as part of the church's mission.

9. The Urgency of the Evangelistic Task

More than 2,700 million people, which is more than two-thirds of mankind, have yet to be evangelized. We are ashamed that so many have been neglected; it is a standing rebuke to us and to the whole church.

There is now, however, in many parts of the world an unprecedented receptivity to the Lord Jesus Christ. We are convinced that this is the time for churches and parachurch agencies to pray earnestly for the salvation of the unreached and to launch new efforts to achieve world evangelization. A reduction of foreign missionaries and money in an evangelized country may sometimes be necessary to facilitate the national church's growth in self-reliance and to release resources for unevangelized areas. Missionaries should flow ever more freely from and to all six continents in a spirit of humble service. The goal should be, by all available means and at the earliest possible time, that every person will have the opportunity to hear, understand, and receive the good news.

We cannot hope to attain this goal without sacrifice. All of us are shocked by the poverty of millions and disturbed by the injustices which cause it. Those of us who live in affluent circumstances accept our duty to develop a simple lifestyle in order to contribute more generously to both relief and evangelism.

10. EVANGELISM AND CULTURE

The development of strategies for world evangelization calls for imaginative pioneering methods. Under God, the result will be the rise of churches deeply rooted in Christ and closely related to their culture.

Culture must always be tested and judged by Scripture. Because man is God's creature, some of his culture is rich in beauty and goodness. Because he is fallen, all of it is tainted with sin and some of it is demonic. The Gospel does not presuppose the superiority of any culture to another, but evaluates all cultures according to its own criteria of truth and righteousness, and insists on moral absolutes in every culture.

Missions have all too frequently exported with the Gospel an alien culture, and churches have sometimes been in bondage to culture rather than to Scripture. Christ's evangelists must humbly seek to empty themselves of all but their personal authenticity in order to become the servants of others, and churches must seek to transform and enrich culture, all for the glory of God.

11. EDUCATION AND LEADERSHIP

We confess that we have sometimes pursued church growth at the expense of church depth, and divorced evangelism from Christian nurture. We also acknowledge that some of our missions have been too slow to equip and encourage national leaders to assume their rightful responsibilities. Yet we are committed to indigenous principles, and long that every church will have national leaders who manifest a Christian style of leadership in terms not of domination but of service.

We recognize that there is a great need to improve theological education, especially for church leaders. In every nation and culture there should be an effective training program for pastors and laymen in doctrine, discipleship, evangelism, nurture and service. Such training programs should not rely on any stereotyped methodology but should be developed by creative local initiatives according to biblical standards.

12. SPIRITUAL CONFLICT

We believe that we are engaged in constant spiritual warfare with the principalities and powers of evil, who are seeking to overthrow the church and frustrate its task of world evangelization. We know our need to equip ourselves with God's armor and to fight this battle with the spiritual weapons of truth and prayer. For we detect the activity of our enemy, not only in false ideologies outside the church, but also inside it in false gospels which twist Scripture and put man in the place of God. We need both watchfulness and discernment to safeguard the biblical Gospel.

We acknowledge that we ourselves are not immune to worldliness of thought and action, that is, to a surrender to secularism. For example, although careful studies of church growth, both numerical and spiritual, are right and valuable, we have sometimes neglected them. At other times, desirous to ensure a response to the Gospel, we have compromised our message, manipulated our hearers through pressure techniques, and become unduly preoccupied with statistics or even dishonest in our use of them. All this is worldly. The church must be in the world; the world must not be in the church.

13. FREEDOM AND PERSECUTION

It is the God-appointed duty of every government to secure conditions of peace, justice and liberty in which the church may

obey God, serve the Lord Christ, and preach the Gospel without
interference. We therefore pray for the leaders of the nations and
call upon them to guarantee freedom of thought and conscience,
and freedom to practice and propagate religion in accordance
with the will of God and as set forth in The Universal Declara-
tion of Human Rights.

We also express our deep concern for all who have been
unjustly imprisoned, and especially for our brethren who are
suffering for their testimony to the Lord Jesus. We promise to
pray and work for their freedom. At the same time we refuse to
be intimidated by their fate. God helping us, we too will seek to
stand against injustice and to remain faithful to the Gospel,
whatever the cost. We do not forget the warnings of Jesus that
persecution is inevitable.

14. THE POWER OF THE HOLY SPIRIT

We believe in the power of the Holy Spirit. The Father sent
his Spirit to bear witness to his Son; without his witness ours is
futile. Conviction of sin, faith in Christ, new birth and Christian
growth are all his work.

Further, the Holy Spirit is a missionary Spirit; thus evangelism should arise spontaneously from a Spirit-filled church. A
church that is not a missionary church is contradicting itself and
quenching the Spirit. Worldwide evangelization will become a
realistic possibility only when the Spirit renews the church in
truth and wisdom, faith, holiness, love and power. We therefore
call upon all Christians to pray for such a visitation of the
sovereign Spirit of God that all his fruit may appear in all his
people and that all his gifts may enrich the body of Christ. Only
then will the whole church become a fit instrument in his hands,
that the whole earth may hear his voice.

15. THE RETURN OF CHRIST

We believe that Jesus Christ will return personally and visibly, in power and glory, to consummate his salvation and his judgment. This promise of his coming is a further spur to our evangelism, for we remember his words that the Gospel must first be preached to all nations. We believe that the interim period between Christ's ascension and return is to be filled with the mission of the people of God, who have no liberty to stop before the End.

We also remember his warning that false Christs and false prophets will arise as precursors of the final Antichrist. We therefore reject as a proud, self-confident dream the notion that man can ever build a utopia on earth. Our Christian confidence is that God will perfect his kingdom, and we look forward with eager anticipation to that day, and to the new heaven and earth in which righteousness will dwell and God will reign forever.

Meanwhile, we rededicate ourselves to the service of Christ and of men in joyful submission to his authority over the whole of our lives.

CONCLUSION

Therefore, in the light of this our faith and our resolve, we enter into a solemn covenant with God and with each other, to pray, to plan and to work together for the evangelization of the whole world.

We call upon others to join us. May God help us by his grace and for his glory to be faithful to this our covenant!

Amen, Alleluia!

BIBLIOGRAPHY

AMONG the books that God's New Envoys may find especially valuable are these:

Miriam Adeney's *God's Foreign Policy* (Grand Rapids: Eerdmans, 1984) is an excellent introduction to the complexities of trying to do good in foreign cultures. Although I would not agree with all of Adeney's evaluations of specific development techniques, I believe her book will give the prospective Envoy valuable insights and an appreciation of the necessity of approaching each culture on its own terms.

Roland Allen's *The Spontaneous Expansion of the Church* (Grand Rapids: Eerdmans, 1984) is a mature work by a very insightful missiologist. First published in 1932, it has withstood the test of time. Although some of Allen's language may seem a little dated, he has brilliant insights into the techniques that make spontaneous expansion work.

God's Smuggler by Brother Andrew and John and Elizabeth Sherrill (Carmel, N.Y.: Guideposts Associates, 1967) is a classic, and deservedly so. As a book about the adventure of missions and the joy of giving one's full trust to the Lord, this volume is hard to beat.

Beyond Hunger by Art Beals with Larry Libby (Portland, Ore.: Multnomah Press, 1985) provides a host of valuable examples of the symbiotic ministry in action. This is good reading for those who are contemplating work with symbiotic ministries—focusing on both physical and spiritual need.

Carl Lawrence's *The Church in China* (Minneapolis: Bethany House, 1985) is full of inspiring stories that demonstrate the true dynamism and miraculous nature of Christ's Church in a highly repressive land.

Norman Rohrer's *This Poor Man Cried* (Wheaton: Tyndale House, 1985) is a true story of a pioneer in the Christian relief and development field, Dr. Larry Ward. It will inspire you, and also help your understanding of the enormity of some of the problems God's New Envoys will face.

Today's Tentmakers by J. Christy Wilson Jr. (Seattle: Overseas Counseling Service, 1979) provides an alternative model for worldwide witness. Just as the apostle Paul financed his own ministry by tentmaking, today's tentmakers can make an invaluable contribution to world evangelization, being free to reach behind closed doors, and easing financial burdens upon the Church.

Other works consulted in preparation of this book:

BOOKS

Aldrich, Joseph C. *Life-Style Evangelism*. Portland, Ore.: Multnomah Press, 1981.

Andrew, Brother. *The Ethics of Smuggling*. Wheaton: Tyndale House, 1974.

Barrett, David B. (ed.). *World Christian Encyclopedia: A Comparative Study of Churches and Religions in the Modern World, AD 1900 to 2000*. Nairobi: Oxford University Press, 1982.

Dayton, Edward R., and Wilson, Samuel. (eds.). *The Refugees among Us: Unreached Peoples '83*. Monrovia, Calif.: MARC, 1983.

Ending Hunger: An Idea Whose Time Has Come. New York: Praeger Publishers, 1985.

Millham, Doug. *Lake Wales Consultation Manual*. Monrovia, Calif.: MARC, 1986.

Priest, Doug Jr., (ed.). *Unto the Uttermost*. Pasadena: William Carey Library, 1984.

Samovar, Larry A., and Porter, Richard E. *Intercultural Communication: A Reader*. Belmont, Calif.: Wadsworth, 1976.

Stott, John. *Lausanne Occasional Papers Number 3*. Minneapolis: World Wide Publications, 1975.

Towns, Elmer; Vaughan, John N.; and Seifert, David J. *The Complete Book of Church Growth*. Wheaton: Tyndale House, 1981.

Verkuyl, J. *Contemporary Missiology*. Grand Rapids: Eerdmans, 1978.

Ward, Larry. *And There Will Be Famines*. Ventura, Calif.: Gospel Light, 1983.

Wilson, J. Christy. *Introducing Islam*. New York: Friendship Press, n.d.

Yamamori, Tetsunao. *Church Growth in Japan*. South Pasadena, Calif.: William Carey Library, 1974.

_____, and Lawson, E. LeRoy. *Introducing Church Growth*. Cincinnati: Standard Publishing, 1975.

_____, and Lawson, E. LeRoy. *Church Growth: Everybody's Business*. Cincinnati: Standard Publishing, 1975.

_____, and Taber, Charles R., (eds.). *Christopaganism or Indigenous Christianity?* South Pasadena, Calif.: William Carey Library, 1975.

PERIODICALS

The Great Commission Handbook. Evanston, Ill.: Sherman
    Marketing Services, 1984.
International and Intercultural Communication Annual. Vol. 5
    (1979). Falls Church, Va.: Speech Communication As
    sociation.
Leadership. Spring, 1984.
Symbiosis. October 1985.
Urban Mission. Vol. I, No. 3 (1984).
World Christian. January-December 1985.

ARTICLES

Brant, Howard, "Integrating Development with Church Plant-
    ing."
Westergren, Cliff, "Priests on the Street Corners of the World."
Yamamori, Tetsunao, "Toward the Symbiotic Ministry: God's
    Mandate for the Church Today."
_____, "Factors in Church Growth in the U.S., etc."

Another publication that would be helpful for God's New
Envoys is the *Christian Life & Witness Course*—a helpful
first step for those who have never witnessed before. Available from Billy Graham Evangelistic Association, P.O.
Box 779, Minneapolis, MN 55440.

ABOUT THE AUTHOR

Tetsunao Yamamori is president of Food for the Hungry, a Christian relief and development organization currently providing assistance to half a million people in more than a dozen countries. The organization is headquartered in Geneva, Switzerland, with support offices in the United States, Japan, Australia, Norway, and Canada.

Prior to joining Food for the Hungry in 1981, Dr. Yamamori served as professor and director of Intercultural Studies at Biola University, and as vice president of the Institute for American Church Growth. He is a former dean of Northwest Christian College.

Dr. Yamamori is a well-known authority on missiology, church growth, and the symbiotic ministry. He has authored five books and more than thirty articles on these subjects.

Dr. Yamamori holds a B.A. from Northwest Christian College, a B.D. from Texas Christian University, and a Ph.D. (in sociology of religion) from Duke University. He is a member of the American Academy of Religion, the Society for the Scientific Study of Religion, *Conference Internationale de Sociologie Religieuse,* and the American Society of Missiology.

A frequent traveler, Dr. Yamamori visits many of the world's neediest regions each year.

Also by Tetsunao Yamamori:

Church Growth in Japan

Christopaganism or Indigenous Christianity? (edited with Charles R. Taber)

Introducing Church Growth: A Textbook in Missions (with LeRoy Lawson)

Church Growth: Everybody's Business (with LeRoy Lawson)